A Complete G

SOUTH
WALES

Roger Thomas

BWRDD CROESO CYMRU
WALES TOURIST BOARD

JARROLD
PUBLISHING

A Complete Guide to

SOUTH WALES

Contents

Features appear in the gazetteer section on the following subjects:

Written and edited by Roger Thomas

Additional research/writing by Herbert Williams

Published jointly by Jarrold Publishing, Norwich and the Wales Tourist Board, Cardiff

Copyright © 1997 Jarrold Publishing/Wales Tourist Board. All rights reserved

Designed by PTP Design Group, Cardiff

Printed by Stephens and George, Merthyr Tydfil

Photographs: Wales Tourist Board Photolibrary, Cadw-Welsh Historic Monuments, National Museums and Galleries of Wales

ISBN 0-7117-0990-4

Jarrold Publishing, Whitefriars, Norwich NR3 1TR

Wales Tourist Board, Brunel House, 2 Fitzalan Road, Cardiff CF2 1UY

Tourist Information Centres

The Wales Tourist Board's TIC network will help you get the most out of your visit to South Wales. TICs are an invaluable source of information on what to do and where to go. 'What's on' events information is also available, together with a wide range of tourist literature. In addition, all Wales Tourist Board TICs operate a bed-booking service (free for local reservations, £1 fee for further afield).

Normal opening times are 10am–5.30pm. These hours may vary to suit local circumstances. Those marked with an asterisk (*) are open seasonally only (April–September).

Abergavenny
Swan Meadow, Monmouth Road, Abergavenny NP7 5HH
Tel (01873) 857588

Barry Island *
The Promenade, The Triangle, Barry Island CF62 5TQ
Tel (01446) 747171

Brecon
Cattle Market Car Park, Brecon LD3 9DA
Tel (01874) 622485

Broad Haven*
National Park Car Park, Broad Haven SA62 3JH
Tel (01437) 781412

Caerleon *
5 High Street, Caerleon NP6 1AG
Tel (01633) 422656

Caerphilly
Lower Twyn Square, Caerphilly CF83 1XX
Tel (01222) 880011

Cardiff
Central Station, Cardiff CF1 1QY
Tel (01222) 227281

Cardigan
Theatr Mwldan, Bath House Road, Cardigan SA43 2JY
Tel (01239) 613230

Carmarthen
Lammas Street, Carmarthen SA31 3AQ
Tel (01267) 231557

Chepstow
Castle Car Park, Bridge Street, Chepstow NP6 5EY
Tel (01291) 623772

Crickhowell *
Beaufort Chambers, Beaufort Street, Crickhowell NP8 1AA
Tel (01873) 812105

Cwmcarn *
Visitor Centre, Cwmcarn Forest Drive, nr Cross Keys NP2 7FA
Tel (01495) 272001

Fishguard Harbour *
Passenger Concourse, The Harbour, Goodwick, Fishguard SA64 0BU
Tel (01348) 872037

Fishguard Town
4 Hamilton Street, Fishguard SA64 9HL
Tel (01348) 873484

Haverfordwest
Old Bridge, Haverfordwest SA61 2EZ
Tel (01437) 763110

Llandarcy *
BP Club, Llandarcy, Neath SA10 6HJ
Tel (01792) 813030

Llandeilo *
Car Park, Crescent Road
Tel (01558) 824226

Llandovery
Heritage Centre, King's Road, Llandovery SA20 0AW
Tel (01550) 720693

Llanelli
Public Library, Vaughan Street, Llanelli SA15 3AS
Tel (01554) 772020

Magor
First Services and Lodge, Junction 23a M4, Magor NP6 3YL
Tel (01633) 881122

Merthyr Tydfil
14a Glebeland Street, Merthyr Tydfil CF47 8AU
Tel (01685) 379884

Milford Haven *
94 Charles Street, Milford Haven SA73 2HL
Tel (01646) 690866

Monmouth *
Shire Hall, Agincourt Square, Monmouth NP5 3DY
Tel (01600) 713899

Mumbles *
Oystermouth Square, Mumbles, Swansea SA3 4DQ
Tel (01792) 361302

Narberth *
Town Hall, Narberth SA67 7AR
Tel (01834) 860061

Newcastle Emlyn *
Market Hall, Newcastle Emlyn SA38 9AE
Tel (01239) 711333

Newport
Museum and Art Gallery, John Frost Square, Newport NP9 1HZ
Tel (01633) 842962

Newport (Pembrokeshire)
2 Bank Cottages, Long Street, Newport SA42 0TL
Tel (01239) 820912

Pembroke *
Visitor Centre, Commons Road, Pembroke SA71 4EA
Tel (01646) 622388

Pembroke Dock *
The Guntower, Front Street SA72 6JZ
Tel (01646) 622246

Penarth *
Penarth Pier, The Esplanade, Penarth CF64 3AU
Tel (01222) 708849

Pont Abraham
Pont Abraham Services, Junction 49 M4, Llanedi SA4 1FP
Tel (01792) 883838

Pont Nedd Fechan *
nr Glyn Neath SA11 5NR
Tel (01639) 721795

Pontypridd
Historical and Cultural Centre, Old Bridge, Pontypridd CF37 4PE
Tel (01443) 409512

Porthcawl *
Old Police Station, John Street, Porthcawl CF36 3DT
Tel (01656) 786639

St David's
City Hall, St David's SA62 6SD
Tel (01437) 720392

Sarn
Sarn Park Services, Junction 36 M4, nr Bridgend CF32 9SY
Tel (01656) 654906

Saundersfoot *
The Barbecue, Harbour Car Park, Saundersfoot SA69 9HE
Tel (01834) 813672

Swansea
Singleton Street, Swansea SA1 3QG
Tel (01792) 468321

Tenby
The Croft, Tenby SA70 8AP
Tel (01834) 842402

Brecon Beacons National Park Information Centres

Brecon Beacons Mountain Centre, nr Libanus, Brecon LD3 8ER   Tel (01874) 623366

Craig-y-nos Country Park, Penycae, Upper Swansea Valley SA9 1GL   Tel (01639) 730395

Also at Abergavenny, Brecon and Llandovery TICs (see above list).

Pembrokeshire Coast National Park Information Centres

40 High Street, Haverfordwest   Tel (01437) 760136

8a Castle Terrace, Pembroke   Tel (01646) 682148

Also at Broad Haven, Newport, St David's and Tenby TICs (see above list).

Where To Go – At a Glance

For quick, easy reference, here's a list of all the attractions and places to visit featured in this book together with the pages on which you'll find the relevant information.

4

Key to Symbols

 Tourist Information Centre

E5 Each entry has a map reference to enable you to locate it on the gridded South Wales map in the back of the book

C/F (Follows telephone number). Admission is charged/free. Please note that for some entries (eg cathedrals) it is not appropriate to include C/F information

 Cadw-Welsh Historic Monuments site

 National Museums & Galleries of Wales

 National Trust

Places to visit

Aberavon

Aquadome at the Afan Lido
Tel (01639) 871444 C
Exciting leisure theme pool with wave machine, water slides, space whirl and Inca temple.

Nearby
Margam Abbey Stones Museum
(located alongside Abbey Church of St Mary, just outside Margam Park) F
Fascinating collection of early Christian and pagan stones, including Cantusus Stone, originally Roman milestone of 4th century.

Margam Country Park
Tel (01639) 881635 C
Very popular family attraction with wide range of activities. Spacious grounds with farm and mountain bike trails, nature reserve, boating lake, fishing, adventure playground, road train, sculptures, giant chess and draughts. Medieval religious ruins and elegant 18th-century orangery. Largest fallow deer herd in South Wales and rare breeds including Iron Age pigs, Vietnamese pigs and Glamorgan cattle. One of the world's largest hedge mazes. Fairytale Land Village for under-eights, with nursery rhyme characters and midget houses.

South Wales Gazetteer

The A–Z gazetteer of resorts, cities, towns and villages starts here. It's all laid out in an informative, easy-to-follow style. Each entry contains a description of the destination in question. Then along the margins you'll find details of the local attractions and places to visit, large and small, mainstream and unusual.

It's impossible, in a guide of this nature, to give precise opening details for each attraction. The vast majority will be open at all reasonable hours from April to the end of September. Many will also stay open (often on a limited basis) in the winter months. Telephone numbers are provided, so you can check for yourself – or call into a Tourist Information Centre for details of the places to visit locally.

The orangery, Margam Country Park

Aberavon
Map Ref **E5**

The seaside resort of Aberavon, with its extensive sweep of firm sands and 2-mile promenade, offers good bathing and surfing and is popular with day visitors. The Afan Lido on the promenade is a major sports and leisure complex. Aberavon, once a borough in its own right, is now part of the steelmaking town of Port Talbot. The town, which stretches along a comparatively narrow strip of land between the mountains and the sea, is close to extensive areas of forest and moorland.

Port Talbot is named after the wealthy Talbot family, who developed the local docks in the 19th century. They lived at Margam Castle, a Gothic mansion built in the grounds of a medieval Cistercian abbey 2 miles east of Port Talbot. The building, with its highly ornamental exterior, is now the centrepiece of a superb country park. This includes an 18th-century orangery of Classical design and the remains of the abbey chapter house.

Margam Country Park

Aberdare

Map Ref **F4**

Coal and iron fuelled the 19th-century growth of Aberdare. Today, the town is a busy shopping centre, surrounded by lofty mountainsides which bear little evidence of Aberdare's industrial past. The town stands at the head of the Cynon Valley. It occupies a broad vale, giving Aberdare's surrounds a sense of spaciousness and openness not usually found in the confines of the South Wales Valleys.

These qualities are seen to good effect at the Dare Valley Country Park, on the western outskirts of the town. Large areas of grassland, open heath, lakes, a cascade and country paths occupy a hillside which was once covered by colliery head-gears and mining waste. Call in first at the visitor centre.

Closer to the town centre is Aberdare Park, a traditional town parkland with a boating lake, woods and swooping meadows.

Places to visit

Aberdare

Dare Valley Country Park
Tel (01685) 874672 F
194-hectare (480-acre) park opened in 1973 on reclaimed land. Walking, fishing, birdwatching, ranger service. Visitor centre has Valley Inheritance Centre with exhibitions, audio-visual theatre.

Abergavenny

Map Ref **G4**

Prosperous Abergavenny is a mixture of traditional and modern. The town, at the gateway to the Brecon Beacons National Park but also close to commercial and industrial South Wales, is a popular residential area. Yet it still retains the look and atmosphere of a country and market town, especially on Tuesdays when the livestock pens in the market place are packed with sheep and the streets are filled with farming folk.

Weekend craft and antique fairs are held regularly in the covered market, part of a grand Victorian Town Hall standing at one end of Abergavenny's long, pleasant main shopping street. The building also houses the excellent Borough Theatre. Just behind the town centre, in peaceful green fields beside the River Usk, stand the ruins of Abergavenny Castle. This was the scene of an infamous deed in 1175 when the Norman lord, William de Braose, invited local Welsh leaders to a banquet, only to murder them while they were disarmed.

Most of what now survives of the castle dates from the 13th and 14th centuries. The gatehouse was probably added in the 15th century. The castle's 19th-century hunting lodge contains a good local museum dedicated to Abergavenny's long history.

In this town, you are never far from greenery. Abergavenny stands almost in the shadow of the 596m (1955ft) Sugar Loaf and 486m (1596ft) Skirrid-fawr mountains. The sheltered Usk Valley and leafy towpaths of the Monmouthshire and Brecon

Abergavenny is surrounded by beautiful landscapes

Canal thread their way through neighbouring parklands. And in the town itself, there are the pretty Linda Vista Gardens and Bailey Park, the latter with extensive leisure facilities.

Places to visit

Abergavenny

Abergavenny Castle and Museum
Tel (01873) 854282 C
Museum contains Welsh farmhouse kitchen and saddler's shop. Regular temporary exhibitions.

Hill Court Gallery, Pen-y-Pound
Tel (01873) 854180 F
Paintings, drawings and limited-edition prints.

Amroth

Colby Woodland Garden
Tel (01834) 811885 C
Walled garden, kitchen garden, Gothic gazebo, wooded paths.

Amroth

Amroth
Map Ref **C4**

The Pembrokeshire Coast National Park starts – or finishes, depending on your direction of travel – at Amroth, a little resort on Carmarthen Bay near Tenby. Amroth is ideal for the quieter style of seaside holiday. It's a little village strung out beside a long beach of firm, gently shelving sands, where you can sometimes see the remains of an ancient forest at low tide. The locals here swear that the south-facing location and shallow waters result in sea temperatures which are warmer than anywhere else along this coast.

The Pembrokeshire Coast Footpath runs for over 180 miles between Amroth and St Dogmael's, near Cardigan. East of Amroth there's a shorter walk – a mere ¾ mile, but long enough to discourage most – to Marros Sands, a perfect away-from-it-all beach. The woods above Amroth contain the Colby Woodland Garden, with its seasonal displays of daffodils, rhododendrons and azaleas.

Angle
Map Ref **A5**

Angle is at the end of the road, but well worth the journey. The village, perched at the mouth of the Milford Haven waterway, can be reached along the B4320 from Pembroke. There are panoramic views across the Haven – and its petro-chemical complexes – from this high-ridged road on the approach to Angle. Look out too for the unusual Rocket Cart House, a house-cum-tower beside the road which was once a lookout and storage point for rescue rockets.

Peaceful Angle was once a busy sea-trading and fishing centre (there is a tiny Fishermen's Chapel behind St Mary's Church). Holiday sailors now use its two harbours at West Angle Bay and the more sheltered Angle Bay to the east. There are lovely views across this latter bay from the unmade road which leads from the village to Old Point House, a waterside inn. West Angle Bay has a good sandy beach and splendid views across the mouth of the Haven to the Dale Peninsula. Thorn Island, just offshore, has a 19th-century fort which now serves as a hotel.

Barry Island

Barry Island

Barry Castle, Park Road F
Remains of 13th-century stronghold of de Barri family. Part of gatehouse still stands, with entrance arch and portcullis grooves. Follow signs to Porthkerry Country Park – you'll see castle at roadside a short distance from park entrance.

Barry Island Pleasure Park
Tel (01446) 732844
Centrepiece of Island – colourful, noisy, exciting. More than 50 rides, including log flume. Prides itself on keeping up with newest attractions. Great place to take kids.

Barry Island/Barry
Map Ref **G6**

Barry Island has been synonymous with seaside fun for generations. It's bright and uncomplicated, with glittering amusement arcades and a cheerful pleasure park full of whirling rides. What's more, there's a superb crescent of south-facing sands along Whitmore Bay, a beach protected by two headlands where bucket-and-spade activity is

Places to visit

Barry Island

Barry Island Steam Heritage Centre
Tel (01446) 748816 C
Railway heritage centre sited in historic station buildings. Photographs and exhibits from the 'Age of Steam'; explains why Barry owes its existence to the railways. Train rides on special 'Steam Days'.

Cold Knap Roman Building
The Knap F
Foundations of supply depot near sea built late in 3rd century when Irish pirates were raiding coast. It's behind fence just above car parking spaces overlooking storm beach at The Knap.

Living Archive Centre for Barry and the Vale, Gladstone Road
Tel (01446) 722166 C
Exhibition centre on past life of Barry and Vale of Glamorgan.

Porthkerry Country Park
Tel (01446) 733589 F
Unusually varied, with seashore, woods and meadows and tall railway viaduct built in 1898. Pleasant short walk past pitch-and-putt course to pebble beach overlooked by massive limestone cliffs.

Nearby
Dyffryn Gardens (on minor road 3½ miles north-west of Barry Island)
Tel (01222) 593328 C
One of Wales's finest landscaped gardens in 28 hectares (70 acres) of parkland around Dyffryn House, a palatial mansion built in 1893. Rare and exotic plants and trees, themed gardens, water lily canal, children's play area.

St Lythans Burial Chamber F
Capstone balanced on stones nearly 3m (10ft) high. Stands in field alongside country lane between Dyffryn Gardens and St Lythans village, near Wenvoe.

Tinkinswood Burial Chamber F
Megalithic chamber for communal burial, dating from around 4000BC. Capstone of 40.6 tonnes believed to be largest in Britain. Take road from St Nicholas to Dyffryn Gardens; signpost after about 915m (1000 yards) points way across fields.

Welsh Hawking Centre and Children's Animal Park
Tel (01446) 734687 C
Attractively laid out in countryside just outside Barry, alongside A4226 (signposted Bridgend). Hawks of all kinds, including kestrel, merlin, eagle owl, snowy owl, peregrine falcon. 'Petting' zoo where children can see rabbits, goats, etc at close quarters. Daily flying displays.

popular. There's a pleasant walk on Barry Island along the grassy headland that runs beside the main beach.

Barry's quieter side lies to the west, along the seafront known as The Knap. This is a restful area with a boating lake, gardens and pebble beach.

Barry's 'island' is in reality a peninsula jutting out from a town that owes its existence to the rows between rival coal barons late in the 19th century. Barry was a tiny hamlet scarcely rating a place on the map before David Davies of Llandinam, Wales's supreme 'self-made man' of the Victorian era, spearheaded a drive to provide a new port in competition to Cardiff. Barry developed at such astonishing speed that it was soon exporting more coal than Cardiff in the halcyon years before World War I.

The coal trade has gone now and the port trades in a variety of commodities, including bananas. A statue of David Davies – sculpted by Sir Alfred Gilbert, creator of *Eros* in Piccadilly Circus – stands outside the docks' offices.

The town, spread across a low hill, has an air of turn-of-the-century solidity. A pair of British lions stand guard outside the old council offices in the town centre, while a fountain plays nearby.

Dyffryn Gardens

Places to visit

Blackwood
Old Mill, Gelligroes
Tel (01495) 222322/222053
Watermill C **Workshop** F
16th-century watermill and candle workshop in picturesque setting.

Nearby
Pen-y-Fan Pond Country Park, nr Oakdale F
Small lake set in high moorland. Good walking country. Wild ponies. Take B4251 to Oakdale off A472 Pontllanfraith–Pontypool road, looking out for signpost at Penyfan Industrial Estate.

Stuart Crystal, Aberbargoed
Tel (01443) 820044 F
Guided tours of factory. Crystal glass blowing and decorating. Factory shop. Take A4049 Pontllanfraith–Rhymney road, look out for signpost in Aberbargoed.

Blackwood
Map Ref **G5**

Blackwood is a busy small town, one of a network of communities in the western valleys of Gwent which were once dependent on coalmining. The smart pedestrianized shopping centre symbolizes the town's faith in its future. On Fridays and Saturdays there is a lively street market. The town is surrounded by green, open hillsides and mountaintops, partly forested, where walking is popular.

Places to visit

Blaenafon

Big Pit Mining Museum
Tel (01495) 790311 C
Gives a complete picture of the life of a South Wales miner. In addition to underground visit, there's lots to see on the surface.

Blaenafon Ironworks
Tel (01495) 792615 C
One of Europe's best-preserved 18th-century ironworks with blast furnaces etc.

Pontypool and Blaenafon Railway
Tel (01495) 792263 C
Standard-gauge steam trains run on ¹/₂-mile section of track just north of Big Pit (open Sundays and Bank Holidays only in season).

Blaenafon

Map Ref **G4**

Coal and iron dominated Blaenafon's past – and coal and iron are still playing a role, though in a very different way. The local coalmine and ironworks are open, though not in their original productive capacity. Big Pit, which closed as a working mine in 1980, is now open to visitors as a mining museum. The surface workings of the coalmine – its engine house, miners' baths and workshops – are intact and accessible, and there is a mining gallery which illustrates methods of coal extraction.

But the highlight at Big Pit is the real thing – the underground guided tour, conducted by ex-miners, to the actual coalface and stables where the pit ponies were kept.

For this, visitors are equipped with miner's helmet and battery before descending 90m (300ft) by pit cage to pit bottom.

Blaenafon Ironworks, dating from 1789, is also open to visitors. A bank of well-preserved blast furnaces, water balance lift and workers' cottages can be seen at this historically important site.

Big Pit Mining Museum

Broad Haven, near Bosherston

Bosherston

Map Ref **B5**

This little village, spread out beside its Norman cruciform church, is bordered by the lovely Bosherston Lakes. The lakes – three long fingers of water – are man-made, created in the late 18th century as part of a country estate. The waters, which spear through thick woodlands, are a sheltered haven for a wide variety of birds. The lakes are at their most attractive in June, when they are covered in waterlilies.

Follow the lakeside path to the small dam which separates fresh – from salt-water. Beyond lies beautiful Broad Haven beach, a stretch of sands sheltered by the cliffs of St Govan's Head. Follow the coast path south-westwards to the headland and St Govan's Chapel, an ancient religious site in an amazing location tucked in amongst the sea rocks.

Places to visit

Bosherston

Nearby
St Govan's Chapel F
Tiny chapel at the base of the cliffs, accessible by steep steps. Mainly 13th century, though dating from 6th century. Probably named after an Irish missionary.

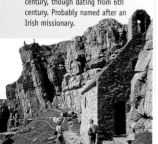

Brechfa

Map Ref **D3**

The Brechfa Forest, one of the largest conifer plantations in Wales, dwarfs tiny Brechfa. The village stands in peaceful countryside at the southern edge of the forest, beneath the open moors of Mynydd Llanybydder.

This haven of tranquillity is an excellent fishing centre. Nearby is the Cothi, a river which yields good catches of salmon and sewin (sea-trout). The woodlands of the Brechfa Forest can be explored by following waymarked paths from the village of Abergorlech 5 miles to the north-east or the Byrgwm picnic site between Brechfa and Abergorlech.

The Brecon Jazz Festival

Brecon

Map Ref **F3**

Narrow streets and passageways, handsome buildings, riverside promenade, hilltop castle and cathedral, livestock mart and covered market are the ingredients that give Brecon its charm. The town is full of character; it's a place untouched by the blight of dreary 20th-century town planning, standardized shopping precincts and boxy architecture.

Go first to The Bulwark, the spacious town square lined with splendid Georgian buildings and dominated by a statue of Wellington. Brecon's Guildhall of 1770 is just along the street, and in the other direction stands the former Shire Hall, a white-stoned Classical structure – complete with imposing portico – which houses the

Places to visit

Brecon
Brecknock Museum
Tel (01874) 624121 C
Love spoons, rural bygones, Roman artefacts. Best exhibit of all is the old assize court, preserved in its full glory.

Brecon Castle F
Curtain wall and tower in grounds of Castle Hotel.

Brecon Cathedral
Historic religious site. Became a cathedral in 1923. A Heritage Centre (tel 01874-625222; C) sited in restored 16th-century tithe barn within the cathedral close contains model of the cathedral, historic exhibits and audio-visual displays.

Jazz Gallery
Tel (01874) 625557 F
Audio-visual and other material tell the story of Jazz and its links with Brecon.

South Wales Borderers' Museum
Tel (01874) 613310 C
Military museum packed with exhibits.

Welsh Distillers Visitor Centre, Parc Menter
Tel (01874) 622926 C
Wales's only whisky distillery explains the history of Welsh whisky in an entertaining way, with talking whisky cask, valley of secret herbs and robotic Celtic monk. Includes tasting.

Nearby
Brecon Beacons Mountain Centre (signposted off A470 at Libanus south of Brecon)
Tel (01874) 623366 F
National park visitor centre. Best starting point for any exploration of Brecon Beacons. In lovely position on Mynydd Illtyd common overlooking central peaks.

Water Folk Canal Centre, Llanfrynach
Tel (01874) 665382 C
Attractive old building beside Monmouthshire and Brecon Canal contains inland waterway memorabilia. Boat trips.

Y Gaer Roman Fort
(2¹⁄₂ miles west of Brecon on minor road next to Y Gaer Farm) F
Once an important Roman stronghold. Evocative ruins with gateways and walls hidden in farmer's fields.

The River Usk flows through Brecon

Places to visit

Bridgend

Newcastle F

Small 12th-century castle, with rare example of elaborately decorated gateway of that period. Off A4063 Maesteg road; hard to locate.

Nearby
Bedford Park, Cefn Cribwr, nr Kenfig Hill
Tel (01656) 725155 F
Park centred on former 18th-century ironworks. Nature trails, industrial archaeology, children's play areas.

Bryngarw, near Bridgend

Bryngarw Country Park
Tel (01656) 725155 F
Woodlands, pastures and formal gardens, including delightful Oriental Garden, make up a varied landscape in grounds of 18th-century Bryngarw House (house has a shop, restaurant and functions suite). Visitor centre, children's play area. Take A4061 for Bryncethin and follow country park signs.

Coity Castle F
Reputedly founded by Payn de Turbeville, one of earliest Norman knights in South Wales. Built in stages from 12th century on and with many interesting features. Pleasantly sited in Coity village, off A4061 north of Bridgend.

Ewenny Priory F
Unusual fortified religious site. Some remains of 12th-century foundation, with beautiful Priory Church alongside. Interesting epitaph to local man killed in American Civil War near pathway in churchyard.

Brecknock Museum. A second museum is located along the tree-lined Watton. This museum, dedicated to the South Wales Borderers, is packed full of military memorabilia, including items from the Zulu War and the regiment's celebrated defence of Rorke's Drift. Brecon's third exhibition space, the Jazz Gallery, is even more unexpected – until you discover that the town holds a famous international jazz festival each summer which attracts top artists from all over the world.

The town stands at the heart of the Brecon Beacons National Park, just a short distance from the highest peaks in South Wales. Despite its obvious appeal to visitors, Brecon remains a working country town – as you'll see if you arrive on a Tuesday or a Friday, when the streets are packed with farmers attracted by the livestock market.

The peaceful side of Brecon, away from the shops and the hustle and bustle, can be found on the hill above the town. Originally, the hill was crowned by a substantial medieval fortification; but time – and road-builders – have not been kind to Brecon Castle, which is now cut in two by a strip of tarmac. Much of the fortress is now incorporated into the frontage of the Castle Hotel, while the ruined Ely Tower is stranded in private ground across the road.

The Norman lord Bernard Newmarch founded both the castle and the religious site that was to become Brecon Cathedral. This building, in secluded, wooded grounds, began life as a Benedictine priory in 1100. A substantial edifice, restored in the 1870s, it contains many ancient features, including a Norman font and an Early English chancel arch. Llanddew, a mile or so to the north-east, was once the home of an important religious palace, fragmentary remains of which can still be seen next to the village's old cruciform church.

Back in Brecon, there's a most pleasant walk along The Promenade, which runs beside the Usk from the town's main bridge. It leads past the weir to a boating station and riverside playing fields. At the opposite end of town, along The Watton, is the terminus of the Monmouthshire and Brecon Canal (boat trips are available). Alongside the canal basin stands the attractive new Theatr Brycheiniog.

Brecon's Leisure Centre, at Penlan overlooking the town, has superb facilities including two heated pools, indoor bowls, health and fitness suites and tenpin bowling.

Bridgend

Map Ref **F5**

Bridgend is a busy town about halfway between Cardiff and Swansea, just south of Junction 36 of the M4 (at which there's a Tourist Information Centre). It's like the hub of a wheel, with roads spreading out in all directions. The seaside resort of Porthcawl is only 5 miles away and the dunes of Merthyr Mawr are also within easy reach.

The town grew up around the confluence of three rivers, the Ogmore, Llynfi and Garw. The most historic part of Bridgend is grouped around the church and medieval fortress of Newcastle. Bridgend is now a commercial, shopping and market centre for a wide area and roughly marks the boundary between the fertile, low-lying Vale of Glamorgan to the east and the more varied, rugged countryside around Margam.

The popular Bridgend Recreation Centre is a very well-equipped leisure centre, one of the largest in Wales, with pool, health and fitness suites, bowls and sports hall.

Broad Haven

Map Ref **A4**

Don't confuse this with Broad Haven beach (see Bosherston entry). Broad Haven is an attractive little resort on St Bride's Bay in the far west of Pembrokeshire. Broad Haven has grown up around a break in the cliffs where low-lying countryside leads down to a superb sandy beach. There is an excellent Pembrokeshire Coast National Park Information Centre in the large car park, which contains displays on wildlife and geology.

The narrow road south across the headland leads to Little Haven – as its name implies, much smaller than its big brother – a collection of houses, inns and places to stay clustered around a cove. Druidston Haven, to the north of Broad Haven, is a remote beach below spectacular cliffs. Parking is difficult. The fourth Haven along this largely inaccessible, cliff-backed coast is at Nolton, with its small sandy beach backed by shingle.

Broad Haven

Caerleon's Roman Amphitheatre

Caerleon

Map Ref **H5**

Caerleon, known to the Romans as *Isca*, is an attractive small town on the River Usk just outside Newport. It was one of the three foremost legionary bases in Britain, the others being Chester and York, and also has links with the Arthurian legends. Fact and fancy have become intertwined – people used to think that the huge grassy mound concealing the remains of the Roman amphitheatre was King Arthur's Round Table!

When Gerald of Wales passed this way in 1188, he found the remains of 'immense palaces' still standing. The extent of this important Roman town can still be appreciated, thanks to the patient efforts of archaeologists, notably Sir Mortimer Wheeler, who excavated the amphitheatre in 1926–7. Here 6000 men could be seated

Places to visit

Caerleon

Caerleon Roman Amphitheatre
Tel (01633) 422518 C
Huge oval-shaped arena, with well-preserved entrances. Section of fortress wall alongside.

Caerleon Roman Barracks F
Lowest portion of original Roman masonry visible; circular oven bases.

Caerleon Roman Fortress Baths
Tel (01633) 422518 C
Roman equivalent of our leisure centre. Swimming pool, changing room and part of the cold hall, discovered only in 1964. Mosaic floors, stone washbasin with head of Medusa. Spoken commentaries and computer graphics.

Caerleon Roman Legionary NMGW
Museum
Tel (01633) 423134 C
Host of finds attractively displayed. Life-size models of centurion, standard bearer and legionary soldier.

Ffwrwm Art and Craft Centre
Tel (01633) 430777 F
Based at historic site (main entrance to Roman town). A variety of crafts, art exhibitions.

to watch military training, gladiatorial combat or the baiting of wild animals.

Go next along Fosse Lane to the remains of the barracks which provided accommodation for the Second Augustan Legion, the crack troops who held this frontier post. Then visit the fortress baths, next to the 15th-century Bull Inn. They are on a grand scale and remind us of the importance of the bathhouse as a social and leisure centre to the Romans.

Roman mosaic, Caerleon

Places to visit

Caerphilly
Caerphilly Castle
Tel (01222) 883143 C
Great Hall, reroofed in 1870, hung with heraldic shields; walks around the walls with fine views of water defences; exhibition of castle building.

Nearby
Nantgarw China Works
Tel (01443) 841703 C
World-famous home of collectable early 19th-century porcelain. Restored 18th-century house contains small museum and interpretive centre. Nantgarw-style ceramics on sale.

Caerphilly

Map Ref **G5**

Visitors to Caerphilly – a lively town 8 miles north of Cardiff – are astounded by their first sight of its castle: a vast medieval fortress, which with its restored water defences covers 12 hectares (30 acres). It rivals Windsor in size and ranks as one of the finest examples of military architecture in Europe.

The castle was built in the 13th century by the Marcher lord Gilbert de Clare – 'Gilbert the Red' – to defend his land against attack by the powerful Welsh prince Llywelyn ap Gruffudd. It was begun in 1268 and although partially destroyed by the Welsh in 1270, most of it was completed

Caerphilly Castle has formidable water defences

by 1271. The death of Llywelyn in battle in 1282 effectively ended Welsh resistance to English rule for more than a century, but the castle remained a formidable seat of Anglo-Norman power and the centre of administration of the extensive estates of the de Clares.

The castle is a superb spectacle, with its massive towers and water-filled moat. It was the earliest castle in Britain to employ the concentric principle, a 'ring within ring' system of walls with inner overlooking outer defences. One of its curiosities is a leaning tower which manages to out-lean the world-famous example at Pisa. The present state of the castle owes much to the extensive restoration work carried out by the 3rd and 4th marquesses of Bute, who owned it before it came into State care in 1950.

The town's Tourist Information Centre contains displays on local history and the surrounding countryside.

Caerphilly Mountain, a 271m (889ft) barrier between the town and Cardiff, is a fine vantage point and good walking country. In the valleys to the north-west of Caerphilly is Senghenydd, originally a coalmining community. The Universal Colliery Memorial, along the B4263, is a symbolic pithead wheel marking the site of the colliery where 439 men and boys died in 1913 – Britain's worst pit disaster.

Caerphilly Castle as it would have looked in its prime

The Great Hall, Penhow Castle

Caerwent

Map Ref **H5**

This unpretentious village just off the A48 between Newport and Chepstow was once *Venta Silurum*, 'the market town of the Silures', the tribe conquered by the Romans around AD75 after 25 years' hostilities.

Long sections of a Roman perimeter walls remain together with an excavated temple. A plaque in the church lychgate commemorates a remarkable Victorian civil engineer, Thomas Andrew Walker, who built the Manchester Ship Canal and the Severn railway tunnel.

The Wentwood Forest, in the rolling hills to the north-west, has attractive views, walks and picnic sites, together with an adventure playground.

Caerwent's Roman Walls

Places to visit

Caerwent

Caerwent Roman Walls F
Go to crossroads on Chepstow side of village and climb steps to wall walk.

Nearby
Llanmelin Wood Hillfort F
Pre-Roman camp for Silures, on minor road between Llanvair Discoed and Shirenewton, north of A48. Hard to locate; parking very difficult.

Penhow Castle
Tel (01633) 400800 C
Memorable audio 'Walkman' tour of Wales's oldest lived-in castle. 15th-century Great Hall with minstrels' gallery, restored Norman bedchamber, craft centre.

Market Days

The country comes to town on market day. If you want to experience the bustle and atmosphere of a Welsh market, then plan your visit from the list below. Market days are great social and well as commercial occasions – it's the day in the week when farming folk not only buy and sell livestock, but also catch up on the local gossip.

Livestock Markets

Abergavenny	Tuesday (weekly)
Brecon	Tuesday & Friday (weekly)
Cardigan	Monday (weekly)
Carmarthen	Monday, Wednesday & Thursday (weekly)
Cowbridge	Tuesday (weekly)
Gowerton	Tuesday (weekly)
Haverfordwest	Tuesday (weekly)
Hay-on-Wye	Thursday (weekly)
Llandeilo	Monday (weekly)
Llandovery	Tuesday (weekly)
Llandysul	Tuesday (fortnightly)
Monmouth	Monday & Friday (weekly)
Neath	Wednesday (weekly)
Newcastle Emlyn	Friday (weekly)
Newport	Wednesday (weekly)
Pembroke	Monday (fortnightly)
Sennybridge	Wednesday (weekly)
Talgarth	Friday (weekly)
Talybont on Usk	Thursday (weekly)
Whitland	Tuesday (weekly)

General Markets

There are also many weekly general markets held throughout South Wales, where stallholders set up shop either under cover or in the streets. Some coincide with livestock markets.

Abergavenny	Tuesday & Friday
Blackwood	Friday & Saturday
Brecon	Tuesday & Friday
Bridgend	Monday–Saturday
Brynmawr	Saturday
Cardiff	Monday–Saturday
Cardiff (Bessemer Road)	Sunday
Cardiff (Splott Market)	Sunday
Cardigan	Saturday
Carew (airfield)	Sunday
Carmarthen	Wednesday & Saturday
Chepstow	Sunday
Crickhowell	Thursday
Ebbw Vale	Friday
Fishguard	Thursday
Haverfordwest	Monday–Saturday; also Sunday at Withybush Showground
Hay-on-Wye	Thursday
Llanelli	Thursday & Saturday
Maesteg	Friday
Merthyr Tydfil	Tuesday & Saturday
Monmouth	Friday & Saturday
Neath	Wednesday & Saturday
Newport	Monday–Saturday (indoor), Saturday (outdoor)
Pontypridd	Friday (indoor), Wednesday & Saturday (outdoor)
Porthcawl	Sunday (summer)
Pontypool	Friday
Port Talbot	Monday–Saturday (indoor), Tuesday, Thursday & Saturday (outdoor)
Swansea	Monday–Saturday
Tenby	Every day except Wednesday & Sunday

An Eventful Place

Wales is an eventful country. A full and lively programme of events takes place throughout the year – there's everything from music festivals to medieval pageants, guided walks to country fairs. In a guide of this size, it's impossible to mention them all, or to give specific dates. Please call in at a Tourist Information Centre for the full picture.

We have made brief reference to selected important events under the relevant locations in the gazetteer. Wales's three major annual events are the Llangollen International Musical Eisteddfod, which takes place in North Wales for a week in the first part of July, the Royal Welsh Show, held in Builth Wells, Mid Wales, for four days in late July, and the week-long Royal National Eisteddfod, held at a different location each year in the first part of August.

Caldicot

Map Ref H5

Caldicot is a quiet town 5 miles south-west of Chepstow, near the M4 and the A48. It lies on the fringe of the Gwent Levels, the most extensive ancient fenland in Wales. Narrow lanes run through this reclaimed land, a silent area criss-crossed with ditches and rich in marsh plants and birdlife. The sea was at one time some distance away and what was once dry land lies beneath the waters of the Severn Estuary.

Caldicot is best known for its beautiful castle, which was founded in the 12th century and built in stages over the next 200 years. It fell into disuse but was restored by the Victorian barrister Joseph Cobb, who carefully researched its original appearance. It is now in the hands of Monmouthshire County Council. The castle is a popular venue for medieval banquets.

The fortress stands in the grounds of a tranquil country park with pleasant walks through woodland and gardens where archaeologists have made some exciting Bronze Age finds.

Places to visit

Caldicot

Caldicot Castle
Tel (01291) 420241 C
Audio 'Walkman' tours vividly interpret castle's history. Views across serene countryside and Severn Estuary. One of Nelson's cannons stands in courtyard.

Nearby
Runston Chapel F
Ruined Norman chapel in farmland 1½ miles north of Crick on minor road to Shirenewton. No signpost. Very hard to locate.

The spectacular mountain road between Capel-y-ffin and Hay-on-Wye

Capel-y-ffin

Map Ref G3

Remote Capel-y-ffin, locked away in the Black Mountains and accessible only by narrow road, is the perfect retreat. It was chosen by the charismatic 19th-century religious figure Father Ignatius as the site of a short-lived monastery. Later, the artist Eric Gill lived here.

The road north from Capel-y-ffin climbs up to the Gospel Pass, the second highest road in Wales which skirts the shoulder of 677m (2220ft) Hay Bluff. A word of warning: the route is extremely narrow in places so beware of oncoming traffic, especially on summer weekends. This is popular pony trekking, hang gliding and walking country (the Offa's Dyke Path runs across these mountains). The views from the road's airy summit at 542m (1778ft) are tremendous, looking north-westwards to the remote hills of Mid Wales and north-eastwards to the rolling green fields of England's border country.

Places to visit

Capel-y-ffin

Llanthony Monastery
Ruined church, part of a 19th-century monastery (in private ownership) on hillside above road. Do not confuse with Llanthony Priory 3 miles south-east. View church from outside only.

Cardiff

Map Ref **G5**

Cardiff, with a population of 280,000, is not only the largest city in Wales, but is also its capital. Exciting developments have been taking place here in recent years, making it a cultural, shopping and business centre with far-reaching plans for the future.

The history of Cardiff dates back to the time of the Romans, who built a fort alongside the River Taff. But Cardiff's real story begins with its phenomenal growth as a sea-port in the 19th century. The coal barons in valleys such as the Rhondda needed an outlet for their exports, and Cardiff provided it. At the height of the coal boom, trains loaded with 'black diamonds' stretched for miles along the railways leading into the port, and dozens of ships rode at anchor waiting their turn to enter. This trade declined rapidly after World War I, as markets lost during hostilities were never regained and oil replaced coal as the

Places to visit

Cardiff

Cardiff Bay Visitor Centre
Tel (01222) 463833 F
Award-winning 'Tube', showcase of the dockland regeneration programme. Spectacular views across bay.

Cardiff Castle
Tel (01222) 878100 C
Amazing blend of genuine old ruins – section of Roman wall, Norman stone keep – and pure architectural fantasy. Lavishly decorated rooms created at vast expense to satisfy whims of rich aristocrat. Famous Animal Wall outside.

Cardiff Castle, 1st The Queen's Dragoon Guards Museum
Tel (01222) 222253
(F after castle admission charge) Range of exhibits include life-size models of mounted officer and guardsman. Monty's messages to Desert Rats. Recruiting posters, weapons, uniforms, medals, taped battlefield sounds.

Cardiff Castle The Welch Regiment Museum
Tel (01222) 229367
(F after castle admission charge) Extensive museum with weapons, uniforms, VCs and citations, colours, stuffed heads of regimental goats.

Cardiff International Arena
Tel (01222) 234600
Wales's national exhibition centre, convention and entertainment venue with seating for over 5000.

Chapter Arts Centre, Market Road, Canton
Tel (01222) 399666
F (C for films, theatre, etc) Lively centre staging exhibitions, films, entertainments. Off Cowbridge Road, main road out of city centre going west.

Craft in the Bay, Bute Street
Tel (01222) 484611 C
Wide selection of crafts – ceramics, glass, textiles, jewellery, wood, etc – created by members of the Makers Guild in Wales.

Llandaff Cathedral
Epstein's superb Christ In Majesty sculpture dominates 12th-century cathedral, restored after World War II bombing. Graceful Victorian spire next to 15th-century Jasper Tower. Painting by pre-Raphaelite Dante Gabriel Rossetti inside.

National Museum and Gallery, NMGW
Cathays Park
Tel (01222) 397951 C
Story of Wales from earliest times. Prehistoric scenes recreated. Dinosaur skeletons. Lively displays of animal and plant life geared to capturing children's imaginations. Outstanding art collections including work of French Impressionists (Cézanne, Monet, Van Gogh, etc) and Augustus and Gwen John.

New Theatre
Tel (01222) 878889
Handsomely refurbished Edwardian theatre. Plays, opera, ballet, pantomime. City centre, off Queen Street.

Norwegian Church, Inner Harbour
Tel (01222) 454899 F
Unusual timber building on waterfront, former church for Norwegian seamen. Now a cultural and arts centre and coffee shop.

Oriel Gallery, The Friary
Tel (01222) 399477 F
Spacious modern bookshop often staging exhibitions, poetry readings. City centre, off Queen Street.

The Point, on the corner of Mount Stuart Square
Tel (01222) 499979
Performance and arts venue in the former St Stephen's Church.

St David's Hall
Tel (01222) 878500
Showpiece concert hall and conference centre staging everything from symphony concerts to rock. Fully air-conditioned auditorium seating 2000. Part of St David's Centre complex in heart of city.

Sherman Theatre, Senghenydd Road
Tel (01222) 230451
Comfortable, well-designed theatre staging wide range of productions. Part of university complex north of Queen Street.

Techniquest, Stuart Street
Tel (01222) 475475 C
Science/technology boring? Not here. Range of imaginative toys make it fun for all. Mirrors, holograms, magnets, etc. Discovery Room, Planetarium and Science Theatre. Sited in Inner Harbour of Cardiff Bay.

Wales National Ice Rink, Hayes Bridge Road
Tel (01222) 397198 C
Every level of ability catered for, from speed skaters to family sessions. Home of highly successful Cardiff Devils ice hockey team.

Welsh Industrial and Maritime Museum, Bute Street NMGW
Tel (01222) 481919 C
Imaginative complex with indoor and outdoor exhibits telling story of industry and transport in Wales. Beam engines, huge colliery ventilating fan, early cars, bikes, railway engines, railway station, tugboat, miniature railway.

Welsh Institute of Sport, Sophia Gardens
Tel (01222) 397571 C
Excellent riverside complex with multi-purpose indoor facilities, shooting range, swimming pool, squash, weight training, astroturf, grass training, tennis courts.

Nearby
Castell Coch, Tongwynlais
Tel (01222) 810101 C
Rub your eyes, but it's real – fairytale-like castle on wooded hillside. Another Bute fantasy – scenes from *Aesop's Fables*, mock medieval paintings. Off A470 to Merthyr Tydfil.

Museum of Welsh Life, St Fagans NMGW
Tel (01222) 573500 C
Vast collection of authentic re-erected buildings including cottages, farmhouses, tollhouse, school, cockpit and chapel, set in beautiful grounds of former manor house. Craftsmen at work, traditional events. 4 miles from city centre.

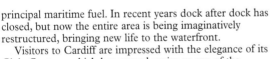

principal maritime fuel. In recent years dock after dock has closed, but now the entire area is being imaginatively restructured, bringing new life to the waterfront.

Visitors to Cardiff are impressed with the elegance of its Civic Centre – which has earned praise as one of the world's finest examples of civic architecture – and the spaciousness of its parks. The neo-Classical civic buildings in Cathays Park, all of white Portland stone, make an impressive architectural collection. They include the City Hall, Law Courts and National Museum of Wales – a trio of fine buildings facing the Boulevard de Nantes – together with the Welsh Office and the Temple of Peace and Health, which was financed by the 1st Lord Davies of Llandinam and embodied his dream of a new international order.

Cardiff Castle, in the very heart of the city, expresses a vision of a different kind – the romantic dreams of the 3rd Marquess of Bute, who in mid-Victorian times hired architect William Burges to turn his fantasies into reality.

The Wales of bygone times at the Museum of Welsh Life

They transformed a genuine Anglo-Norman castle into an extravagant architectural pot-pourri of richly decorated rooms which has immense appeal for all but the most severely pedantic. Peacocks strut its grounds, which seem a world removed from the busy streets outside. The castle can be seen as a combination of whimsy and wealth, the finance for the marquess's architectural indulgences coming from the immense fortune he made in Cardiff's booming docklands. The castle is a venue for medieval banquets.

The Pierhead Building, Cardiff Bay

Cardiff has been sensible enough to retain its canopied shopping arcades which are delightful period pieces, while pressing ahead with the unashamedly modern St David's Centre, Capitol Centre and Queen's Centre, and a bustling new alfresco 'Café Quarter' along Mill Lane. It also has a lively Victorian indoor market where you can buy all kinds of fresh foods including the Welsh delicacy, laverbread. Near the market is the medieval St John's Church, the oldest church in the city. The Roman Catholic Cathedral is not far away in Charles Street, but Llandaff Cathedral (Church in Wales) is 2 miles from the city centre in a peaceful 'village' setting.

A mile of so south of the city centre, a new Cardiff is taking shape in the old docklands. The Cardiff Bay development, one of the largest of its kind in Europe, will give the city a freshwater lake and 8 miles of new waterfront. The scheme is already well advanced: the Inner Harbour, with its attractive promenades and views across the bay to Penarth, has taken on a new life in recent years and attracts many visitors. Clustered around the harbour is a range of attractions, including the Cardiff Bay Visitor Centre, Norwegian Church, Techniquest and the Welsh Industrial and Maritime Museum. The ornate, red-bricked Pierhead Building and nearby Mount Stuart Square, with its imposing Victorian buildings, are reminders that this port was once one of the world's wealthiest.

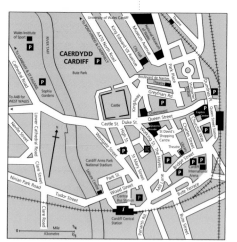

The city is justly proud of its 2000-seater St David's Hall, which stages top-class concerts, and its 5500-seat International Arena. The two main theatres, the New and the Sherman, are supplemented by the Chapter Arts Centre in Canton and The Point in Butetown. The world-famous Welsh National Opera has seasons at the New Theatre.

Cardiff has excellent sporting facilities. Renowned the world over as the spiritual home of rugby, the legendary Cardiff Arms Park is currently being transformed into the striking new Millennium Stadium, scheduled for completion in 1999. The city has league soccer at Ninian Park, county cricket at Sophia Gardens and an impressive ice hockey team. The Welsh Institute of Sport is a mecca offering specialist facilities for training and competition up to the highest level.

Cardiff is also a city of parks and gardens. Don't miss out on a visit to Roath Park, if you can help it – you'll find a large boating lake with a lighthouse-shaped memorial to Scott of the Antarctic (who sailed from Cardiff on his doomed expedition) and superb gardens. Another place not to be missed is the Museum of Welsh Life at St Fagans, a pretty village on the outskirts of the city. The museum recreates bygone times in its collection of old buildings, brought from all parts of Wales, which have been rebuilt stone-by-stone, timber-by-timber, in a beautiful parkland setting.

Cardigan, at the mouth of the River Teifi

Cardigan

Map Ref **C3**

Cardigan is a bright and bustling market town with lots of character. It was once one of the principal ports along the west coast of Wales and although its days of maritime glory are over, much of interest remains. The long main street is remarkable for the variety of its shops and hotels, some of the inns going back to the days of the stagecoach.

Cardigan was granted a royal charter in 1230, but its story begins well before that. This was part of the hotly contested territory of Deheubarth in the days when the Norman invaders came up against the stubborn Welsh princes. The remains of the castle, overlooking the centuries-old stone bridge across the Teifi at the southern approach to the town, are visible proof of the power struggles of that far-distant time. The castle changed hands frequently in the 12th century but was certainly held by the Welsh in 1176, as the powerful Lord Rhys staged the first eisteddfod there.

One of the town's architectural jewels is the old Guildhall, with its arches and clock tower. It is no longer an administrative centre but houses a fascinating array of market stalls. Geoffrey Powell's beautiful sculpture of a Teifi otter, on the town side of the bridge, was presented to Cardigan by David Bellamy. The Welsh Wildlife Centre is located a few miles to the south (see Cilgerran entry). Theatr Mwldan is a community theatre with a lively range of productions.

Places to visit

Cardigan
Canolfan Hanes Aberteifi
Tel (01239) 614404 C
Heritage centre in historic riverside warehouse. Tells story of Cardigan from pre-Norman times to present day.

Cardigan Castle
Scanty remains of a circular keep and two towers. Interior not open to public. View from outside only.

Nearby
Cardigan Island Coastal Farm Park, Gwbert
Tel (01239) 612196 C
On scenic headland overlooking Cardigan Island. Farm animals, sea-birds and breeding colony of grey seals.

St Dogmael's Abbey F
Remains of 12th-century Benedictine abbey attractively sited on hillside. Epitaphs to shipwrecked mariners in adjacent churchyard.

Y Felin, St Dogmael's
Tel (01239) 613999 C
Working watermill producing stoneground flour, opposite abbey. Duckpond at roadside.

Carew Cross

Carew Castle

Places to visit

Carew

Carew Castle
Tel (01646) 651782 C
Handsome fortress in picturesque riverside setting.

Carew Cross F
Highly decorative Celtic cross.

Carew Tidal Mill
Tel (01646) 651657 C
Made ingenious use of tidal waters.

Carew

Map Ref **B4**

There are at least three reasons for visiting Carew – its castle, tidal mill and Celtic cross. The roadside cross will be a familiar sight to anyone travelling around Wales. It has been adopted as the official symbol of Cadw-Welsh Historic Monuments, the heritage body responsible for many of Wales's castles and historic sites. The 11th-century cross, one of the finest in Britain, stands 4m (14ft) high and is decorated with striking patterns. It is a memorial to a Welsh king.

In the fields behind stands the stately shell of Carew Castle. The stronghold, originally Norman, later became a Tudor and Elizabethan residence. This combination of fortress and house is summed up in the architectural counterpoint between the massive medieval round towers and the beautifully carved stonework of the mullioned windows, a later addition.

The castle occupies an idyllic setting beside the tidal waters of the River Carew. Close by, on a causeway which traps the river's high-tide waters, is the Carew Tidal Mill. This four-storeyed building – one of only three restored tidal mills in Britain – has records dating back to the 1550s, though the present mill was constructed in the early 19th century. The mill's complex workings are explained by a self-guided sound system.

Mill, castle and cross are linked by a round walk.

Carmarthen

Map Ref **D4**

Carmarthen is a market town rich in legend and history. For romantics, its chief claim to fame is that it was reputedly the birthplace of the wizard Merlin, whose father was said to be king of the region in the so-called Dark Ages that followed the departure of the Romans. Whether this is so or not (and whether Merlin ever existed) can be endlessly argued, but the town has fed eagerly on the tradition and for years a wizened tree known as Merlin's Oak stood in Priory Street. The tree was removed during road improvements despite the prophesy:

When Merlin's Oak shall tumble down,
then shall fall Carmarthen town.

Pieces of the ancient oak are on display at St Peter's Civic Hall and Carmarthenshire Museum.

Carmarthen

There is no doubt at all surrounding Carmarthen's Roman associations, for it was the site of *Moridunum*, the Romans' most westerly fortress in Britain. Jewellery and other finds can be seen in the museum, but apart from these the only physical evidence of the Romans' presence is a large amphitheatre on the eastern approaches to the town.

In modern times, Carmarthen has made a name for itself as a county town, marketplace and commercial centre for a wide area. For centuries it has lured the farmer and his wife to market, for it is the 'capital' of a region where the predominant industry is agriculture.

Latterly it has responded to the needs of the tourist. Carmarthen has never stood still and has a businesslike air which gives it vitality and colour. The town is at its liveliest on Wednesdays, when the livestock market is in full swing. Old and new live together in perfect compatibility. The modern shopping area and busy indoor market exist side by side with streets and narrow passageways which would be recognizable to the ghosts of long-dead citizens. The architectural variety of the town is a delight, and the maze of streets and alleyways near the castle ruins transports us back through time with only a little imagination.

The Guildhall, with its Classical façade, dates from 1770 and nearby is Nott Square, named after General Sir William Nott, a hero of the Afghan wars of the 1840s. An earlier celebrity, General Sir Thomas Picton, who fell at Waterloo, is commemorated by a tall tapering column at the top of Picton Terrace on the western side of town. Carmarthen's Lyric Theatre stages a regular programme of live performances.

In rolling countryside to the east, the National Botanic Garden of Wales, a multi-million pound Millennium Project opening in phases between 1998 and 2000, promises to attract many visitors.

Town centre, Carmarthen

Carmarthen Heritage Centre

Gwili Railway

Places to visit

Carmarthen

Carmarthen Castle, off Nott Square F
Gatehouse, two towers and bailey remain, but not much else. Mainly 13th century in origin.

Carmarthen Heritage Centre
Tel (01267) 223788 F
Presents the history of Carmarthen as a town and port from AD75 to modern times.

Oriel Myrddin Art Gallery
Tel (01267) 222775 F
Changing exhibitions of contemporary crafts and art.

Roman Amphitheatre, Priory Street F
One of only seven in Britain, unique in construction, the earth excavated for northern seating bank being used to build facing bank. Probably built late in 2nd century. Lack of signposting makes it hard to locate. Look for green slope on left on main road heading east for Llandeilo (A40), before the junction with A484 to Cardigan.

Nearby
Carmarthenshire County Museum, Abergwili (1½ miles away on A40 to Llandeilo)
Tel (01267) 231691 C
Varied and interesting collections in old Bishop's Palace. Roman finds, painted wooden figures from ancient Egypt, stones inscribed with Ogham script, Victorian local bank notes, trade tokens, costumes, military items, charms against witches, man trap, penny-farthing bicycle.

Gwili Railway, Bronwydd (3 miles away on A484 to Cardigan)
Tel (01267) 230666 C
Steam trains run for about 1½ miles on standard gauge to Llwyfan Cerrig along former Great Western Railway branch line. Atmospheric signal box with 21 levers. Refreshments in 1968 BR buffet car.

Nantybwla Farmhouse Cheese Centre
Tel (01267) 237905 C
Cheesemaking demonstrations, museum and shop.

National Botanic Garden of Wales, Middleton Hall (on minor road between Llanarthney and Porth-y-rhyd, 7 miles east of Carmarthen)
Tel (01558) 668768 C
Major Millennium Project, the first modern botanic garden in Britain with conservation as its primary aim. Based at an 18th-century pleasure park with lakes, waterfall and cascades. First phase of the construction programme due for completion in May 1998 includes Great Glasshouse with unique collection of all the mediterranean floras of the world, 'hands on' Bioverse concourse, lakes, rock garden and Welsh habitats.

Paxton's Tower
(accessible from minor road in hills 1 mile south-east of Llanarthney) F
Prominently sited early 19th-century folly, dedicated to Lord Nelson, erected by Sir William Paxton. One time part of the Middleton Hall Estate.

Brecon Beacons
National Park

This 519-square-mile national park stretches from the Wales/England border as far west as Llandeilo. The park's mountain ranges often cause confusion – so let's clear things up once and for all. The national park consists of four ranges, only one of which is called the Brecon Beacons. Starting at the border we have the Black Mountains, followed by the Brecon Beacons which occupy centre ground in the heart of the park. The Beacons are flanked to the west by Fforest Fawr, a moorland wilderness which leads to the Black Mountain (singular!) on Llandeilo's doorstep. Confusing, isn't it?

Perhaps these distinctions are academic, for most visitors are attracted to this national park on the strength of its openness, lack of boundaries and sense of freedom. Mountain range blends into mountain range in a petrified green sea dipping and rising across the landscape, a wave-like effect made all the more emphatic by the mountains' bare, treeless slopes.

The highest point in the park – and South Wales – is Pen-y-fan, an 886m (2907ft) flat-topped summit in the central Beacons. This is the destination which most walkers head for. But there are many other wonderful walking areas – the Offa's Dyke Path in the Black Mountains, for example, or the Sarn Helen Roman road cutting across Fforest Fawr.

A string of reservoirs and stretches of man-made forest are to be found along the southern slopes of the park. Recreational facilities here include waymarked woodland walks and picnic sites.

The park's great outdoors are also popular with pony trekkers, sailors, canoeists, cavers and canal cruisers. The best starting point for any visit is the national park's Brecon Beacons Mountain Centre (open all year) near Libanus, south-west of Brecon. Other national park information centres (some open seasonally) are located at Abergavenny, Brecon, Craig-y-nos Country Park and Llandovery (see Tourist Information Centres on page 3).

No mention of the Brecon Beacons would be complete without reference to the limestone country around the park's southern rim. Most of the park is made up of old red sandstone rock, which has weathered to give the Beacons their distinctive rounded profiles. The outcropping bands of limestone in the south have created a completely different terrain of wooded gorges, caves, pot-holes and waterfalls.

Caswell Bay

Map Ref D5

Caswell is one of the first of the Gower Peninsula's string of south-facing bays on the road west from Swansea. Its spacious sandy beach, fringed by rocky headlands thick with vegetation, is a popular spot. The car park borders the Bishop's Wood Nature Reserve, a sheltered woodland with footpaths, pony trails and picnic sites. There are also splendid cliff walks to Langland Bay and the old smugglers' haunt of Brandy Cove.

Cenarth

Map Ref C3

This tiny village was immortalized by the 12th-century traveller Gerald of Wales (Giraldus Cambrensis), who wrote of the salmon leaping there 'as high as the tallest spear'. There were beavers in the River Teifi then, but you won't find any now.

The flat rocks exposed when the water is low are handy platforms for viewing Cenarth Falls – a much-visited beauty spot since Victorian times – where the Teifi spumes in a series of small descents. Cenarth's handsome three-arch bridge goes back two centuries. St Llawddog's Church has beautiful stained glass and a 5th-century stone in the churchyard, near the porch, with a Latin inscription: *Curcagn-i Fili Andagell* (Curcagnus, son of Andagellus).

Cenarth's working watermill also serves as an interpretive centre where various kinds of coracle – a small one-man boat with a basketwork frame which goes back to pre-Roman times – are on display. Visitors to Cenarth can sometimes see coracles in action on the waters of the Teifi. There is a display of equipment and rural bygones at the Old Smithy, a restored blacksmith's forge and craft shop.

Caswell Bay

Places to visit

Cenarth

National Coracle Centre and Cenarth Mill
Tel (01239) 710980 C
Traces the history of coracle fishing in Wales. Also has examples of coracles from other parts of the world. Tour includes visit to restored 17th-century flour mill.

Nearby
Caws Cenarth Cheese, Fferm Glyneithinog, Penrherber
Tel (01239) 710432 F
Watch the making of traditional farmhouse cheese. Check demonstration times before going.

Chepstow

Map Ref H5

Chepstow, the ancient gateway to Wales, is a fascinating little town which many people miss as they drive along the M48 into Wales after crossing the original Severn Bridge. There was an Iron Age hillfort in the vicinity and the Romans threw a bridge across the Wye ½ mile upstream, but its real history begins with the Norman Conquest. The high bluff commanding the river was of such strategic importance that in 1067, only a year after William of Normandy's invasion, one of his knights, William fitz Osbern, had begun building his Great Tower, which was reputedly the earliest stone castle in Britain. The defences were gradually extended over the succeeding centuries and Chepstow was held for the King at the outbreak of the Civil War. The Great Tower has survived the ages and the castle, even in its ruin, creates an awesome impression of power. There are fine views across the river from the paths inside the castle.

Chepstow has retained its medieval street pattern and Town Gate, built late in the 13th century. This stands at the top of the High Street. Turn right after passing through the gate from the west to see a well-preserved section of the town wall – known as the Portwall – which is roughly the same age as the gate. The main shopping streets slope down to a riverside walk providing views of Brunel's tubular suspension railway bridge of 1852 (alongside the new road bridge) and, a short distance upstream, the fine cast-iron bridge of 1816, which still carries traffic. The Willow Tree riverside restaurant has a plaque recording the

Places to visit

Chepstow
Chepstow Castle
Tel (01291) 624065 C
Well-preserved castle, an excellent illustration of the developing story of fortification over the centuries. Substantial remains include 13th-century gatehouse and Marten's Tower, where regicide Henry Marten was imprisoned for 20 years after the Restoration; Civil War exhibition with life-size figures in battledress and displays of weapons.

Chepstow Museum, Bridge Street
Tel (01291) 625981 C
Attractive displays that bring local history to life. Re-creation of High Street shops in 1920s.

Stuart Crystal
Tel (01291) 620135 F
See craftspeople decorate handmade crystal; museum section showing past and present crystal.

Chepstow, at the gateway to the Wye Valley

transportation to Tasmania from this spot of the Chartist leaders after the abortive march on Newport in 1839.

Chepstow stands at the southern end of the Offa's Dyke Path, a 168-mile borderland walk which runs to Prestatyn in North Wales. The waymarked Wye Valley Walk runs for 52 miles from Chepstow to Hereford. On the outskirts of town is the Chepstow Racecourse.

Places to visit

Cilgerran

Cilgerran Castle
Tel (01239) 615007 C
Castle in spectacular location on crag above the Teifi Gorge.

Welsh Wildlife Centre (on western approach to Cilgerran)
Tel (01239) 621600 C
109-hectare (270-acre) reserve. 5 miles of footpaths cross a variety of habitats, including the second largest reedbed in Wales. Animal farm, conservation garden, tree nursery, adventure playground and futuristic visitor centre. Look out over the reserve from the Tree-Tops Hide. Owned and managed by Dyfed Wildlife Trust.

Nearby
Bro-Meigan Gardens, Boncath
Tel (01239) 841232 C
2½ hectares (6 acres) of formal gardens, varied and attractively landscaped, created out of former smallholding. Marvellous views towards the Preseli Hills.

Shire Horse Farm, Eglwyswrw
Tel (01834) 891640 C
Working farm with horse and tractor rides, play areas, nature trail.

Cilgerran

Map Ref C3

This trim village in the Teifi Valley is justly famous for its castle, which stands on a crag high above the river. Lovers of the romantic relish the tale of how 'the Welsh Helen', Nest – wife of the Norman overlord – was abducted here by a Welsh prince in 1109. The present castle dates from 1223. Its twin towers still have a swaggering and domineering look. Steep flights of stone steps enable the visitor to view their interiors.

Coracle fishermen may sometimes be seen in the vicinity and there is a Coracle Regatta every August.

Cilgerran Castle

Clydach

Map Ref **G4**

This village stands at the foot of the Clydach Gorge, a place of beauty and early industry. Traffic sweeps past on the A465 'Heads of the Valleys' road unaware that shrouded amongst the trees lie the remains of an ironworks dating from the late 18th century. The best starting point for an exploration of the ironworks is the picnic area on the minor road at the foot of the gorge off the A465.

The woodlands in the gorge are splendid – so splendid that its native beechwoods, one of the few surviving in Wales, are now a National Nature Reserve.

Cowbridge

Map Ref **F6**

The prosperous town of Cowbridge stands in the fertile Vale of Glamorgan, the 'Garden of Wales'. The town, its long main street lined with historic buildings, fashionable shops and places to eat, has been the unchallenged 'Capital of the Vale' for centuries. In medieval times it was the walled market town for the Vale. Remnants of the old walls and the narrow gateway known as South Gate or Mill Gate can still be seen to the south of the main shopping street past the church.

Cowbridge is an ideal centre from which to explore the Vale's picturesque villages – with their abundance of thatched cottages – and historic sites. A mile or so to the south-east is Beaupre (pronounced 'bewper') Castle, standing in splendid isolation amongst green fields. It's a pleasant walk of at least ¼ mile from the road, and well worth it, for Beaupre displays many fine features. More a fortified Elizabethan manor house than an out-and-out military site, the castle has such luxurious features as large mullioned windows and two superb Italianate porches, one of which (dated 1586) is decorated with the arms of the Bassets, founders of Beaupre, and their family motto (in Welsh), 'Better death than shame'.

Craig-y-nos

Map Ref **E4**

The irregular outcrops and screes in the green hills above Craig-y-nos signal the presence of limestone rock. The action of water on this limestone over countless thousands of years has created a vast cave system, part of which is open to the public at the Dan-yr-Ogof Showcaves.

The caves were first discovered in 1912, and have yet to be completely explored. At Dan-yr-Ogof, there are three separate cave experiences. The first is the main Showcave, a labyrinthine complex (visitors are allowed into the first ½ mile of a 9-mile system) with spectacular stalagmite and stalactite formations.

Dan-yr-Ogof's Cathedral Cave is named after its central feature, the 'Dome of St Paul's', a vast chamber 13m (42ft) high approached by a long passage. The Bone Cave contains imaginative displays which give a fascinating insight into cave settlement and archaeology. Dan-yr-Ogof has a well-deserved reputation as a top family attraction. The complex also includes a dinosaur park, shire horse centre, museum, dry ski slope and Iron Age farm.

The Craig-y-nos Country Park is almost opposite the caves. This lovely 16-hectare (40-acre) parkland was the 'pleasure grounds' of Craig-y-nos Castle, home of the internationally famous 19th-century opera singer Madame

Places to visit

Cowbridge

Nearby
Beaupre Castle F
Lonely stronghold set amidst pleasant, green fields.

Llanerch Vineyard, Hensol, Pendoylan
Tel (01443) 225877 C
Tours of vineyard producing Wales's only commercially estate-bottled wine. Wine tasting. Also nature trail through woodland.

Dan-yr-Ogof Showcaves

Places to visit

Craig-y-nos

Craig-y-nos Country Park
Tel (01639) 730395 F
Lovely walks, picnic sites. Exhibition in park's visitor centre.

Dan-yr-Ogof Showcaves
Tel (01639) 730284 C
The largest showcaves complex in western Europe. Lots of other attractions (dinosaur park etc) also on this extensive site.

Adelina Patti. The ornamental park, laid out beside the River Tawe, is a beautiful area of meadows, lakelands, fields and woodlands. The castle, an imposing 19th-century 'sham' in typical high Victorian style, contains an outstanding bijou theatre created by Adelina Patti (it is in private ownership but there are occasional guided tours – please telephone 01639-730205). A Brecon Beacons National Park information centre is located at the park.

The Henrhyd Falls tumble through a wooded chasm in the hills to the south near Coelbren.

Crickhowell

Map Ref G4

Pretty Crickhowell stands in the Usk Valley beneath the flat-topped summit of Crug Hywell (Howell's Fort), an Iron Age encampment. The town was a busy staging post in the days of stagecoach travel – the Bear Hotel retains its 'Post Horses' archway and cobbles from those times. Crickhowell's best-known landmark is its long bridge across the Usk, dating from the 16th century. It seems to play a conjuring trick with its length: 13 arches can be seen from its eastern end, while only 12 are visible from the west.

The park contains the ruins of a Norman castle and steep, grassy mound, once an important medieval power base. The tall, needle-sharp spire clearly visible above the rooftops belongs to St Edmund's Church, a 14th-century building with a fine interior. The Georgian house of Gwernvale on the outskirts, now a hotel, was once the home of Sir George Everest, Surveyor-General of India, after whom the world's highest mountain is named.

A little further along the valley is Tretower Court and Castle, an unusual 'two-in-one' historic site. A solid 13th-century round keep, plainly military in design, stands next to a stylish old manor house. The spacious house, noted for its fine woodwork, is an icon of the more settled late Middle Ages when greater consideration could be given to domestic comfort.

To the west of Crickhowell, above the village of Llangattock, are the spectacular cliffs and caves of the Craig y Ciliau Nature Reserve. Hidden in the little-travelled hills to the north-east is lovely Partrishow Church (see Partrishow entry).

Cross Keys

Map Ref G5

This straggling village of mainly terraced houses stands at the southern end of the Ebbw Valley, once clamorous with industry. With the closure of the coalmines that were at the heart of its economy, the essential beauty of the area has been re-established. The steep-sided hills above, now clothed with conifers, lead to open moorlands.

The medieval castle at Tretower

Cwmbran

Map Ref **G5**

Modern Cwmbran – Wales's only 'new town' – has excellent shopping, theatre, sports and leisure facilities. Its international athletics stadium is attached to a leisure centre with multi-use activities, including swimming, squash and sauna. Cwmbran's well-planned shopping centre makes life easy for shoppers. There's plenty of free car parking right next to the shops, and a wide range of retail outlets including big stores.

The Llantarnam Grange Arts Centre, situated in the centre of Cwmbran, holds a varied programme of exhibitions, events and workshops.

Places to visit

Cwmbran

Greenmeadow Community Farm
Tel (01633) 862202 C
61-hectare(150-acre) farm with rare breeds, pet's corner, wildfowl, nature trail, craft workshops.

Llantarnam Grange Arts Centre
Tel (01633) 483321 F
Variety of exhibitions in main gallery.

Cwm-yr-eglwys

Map Ref **B3**

Cwm-yr-eglwys means 'the valley of the church'. Unfortunately, the 12th-century church has seen better days. It was overwhelmed in a huge coastal storm in 1859, leaving only the belfry and part of the wall intact. But the seashore church is not the real reason for visiting this pretty Pembrokeshire village. It stands at the approach to Dinas Island (a headland, not a proper island), whose cliffs and sea-bird colonies can be explored by coastal footpath from the village.

Cwm-yr-eglwys

Cymmer

Map Ref **F5**

If you want to update your image of the South Wales Valleys, then go to Cymmer. This was once a coalmining area, yet has since been called a 'Little Switzerland'. The reason is plain to see. Steep-sided valley slopes are clothed in conifers, not disfigured by spoil heaps. The Afan Argoed Country Park, which occupies an entire mountainside, is a beautiful area which can be explored by foot (waymarked and guided walks) or cycle (bike hire on site).

The South Wales of bygone times is remembered at the Welsh Miners' Museum, also at Afan Argoed. This award-winning museum manages to capture the dignity and the dangers of a coalminer's life in the hectic heyday of the South Wales Valleys. Old photographs, mining equipment, simulated underground workings and a scene from a miner's cottage give visitors a glimpse into the hardships shared by the tightly knit valleys communities.

Pont-rhydyfen, a short distance away, was the birthplace of Richard Burton.

Places to visit

Cymmer

Nearby
Afan Argoed Country Park, Cynonville
Tel (01639) 850564 F
Countryside Centre, forest walks, picturesque riverside.

Welsh Miners' Museum, Afan Argoed Country Park
Tel (01639) 850564 C
The life and times of the South Wales miner.

Afan Argoed Country Park, near Cymmer

Dale

Map Ref **A4**

The sheltered waters off Dale ensure the village's popularity as a sailing and watersports centre. Dale's waterfront cottages look out across a calm, east-facing bay – known as Dale Roads – cradled by protective headlands yet only a short distance from the open seas at the mouth of the Milford Haven waterway. Across the fields ¾ mile to the west there's an entirely different scene. Westdale Bay, a popular surfing beach, is exposed to the full force of the seas.

Sailing at Dale

Dale stands at the approach to the Dale Peninsula, one of the most remote – and loveliest – stretches of the Pembrokeshire Coast National Park, well away from the mainstream of tourist traffic. If you want coastal solitude and spectacular sea views, then walk the coast footpath around the peninsula. At its tip is St Ann's Head, where a coastguard station and marine rescue centre keep a watchful eye over the busy shipping lanes at the entrance to the Milford Haven waterway.

Nearby Mill Bay played a little-known role in an event of great historic significance. Harri Tudur landed here on 7 August 1485. Harri, a Welshman born at Pembroke Castle, marched from Mill Bay to Bosworth Field in the English Midlands, where he achieved a famous victory over Richard III to become Henry VII, founder of the mighty Tudor dynasty.

Dale's earlier history is reflected in its name. The Viking invaders who terrorized these parts during the Dark Age left a legacy of strange-sounding placenames (Skomer, Skokholm, etc) of which Dale, meaning 'valley', is one.

Mill Bay, Dale Peninsula

The peninsula can be one of extremes. It is one of the windiest places in Britain, wind speeds of over 100mph having been recorded here at least five times since 1946. In compensation, it is also the sunniest place in Wales, possibly in Britain, with an annual average of over 1800 hours.

When the sun is out, there's no more idyllic a spot than Watwick Bay on the peninsula's sheltered east coast. The bay, a delicious blend of golden sands, clear seas and green vegetation, takes on a positively Caribbean air on warm summer days.

Places to visit

Dulais Valley

Cefn Coed Colliery Museum, Crynant
Tel (01639) 750556 C
Colliery machinery, mining exhibitions.

Gunsmoke and Seven Sisters Sawmill
Tel (01639) 700288 C
Miniature Gunsmoke Cowboy Town, children's adventure playground, working sawmill, miners' lamp museum.

Dulais Valley

Map Ref **E4**

The hills in this valley on the north-western edge of the South Wales coalfield are surprisingly green. Evidence of past mining activity is now hard to find, unless you visit the Cefn Coed Colliery Museum at Crynant. Based at the Blaenant Colliery, which was one of the last working coalmines in South Wales (it closed in 1990), the museum gives a complete picture of how a mine operated. Highlights include a simulated underground mining gallery and six giant boilers which powered two winding engines, one of which still works by electrical power.

For something completely different, drive up the valley a few miles to Seven Sisters. The sawmills here are the unlikely home of the Gunsmoke Cowboy Town, a re-creation of the Wild West with regular shoot-outs.

Ebbw Vale

Map Ref **G4**

The old iron and steelmaking town of Ebbw Vale was the focus of attention in 1992 as the home of the Garden Festival Wales. A 1½-mile swathe of valley floor, hillside and mountain south of the town was transformed by imaginative landscaping which saw the planting of thousands of trees and the creation of many striking features, including a lake.

It's well worth taking a trip down the valley a mile or so south of Ebbw Vale to see the transformation of an area which was once a derelict industrial eyesore. The site was designed to facilitate a proper after-use, something which other Garden Festivals have lacked, and business, housing and leisure developments have since taken place here. A Festival Park has been created, covering about one-third (26 hectares/65 acres) of the original festival site. Many features from the festival remain, including the lake, Tropical Planthouse, Oriental Pavilion, Woodland and Wetland Centres, 'Mother Earth' sculptures and 'Wave Wall' drystone walling, and there is a visitor centre on site. Festival Park is also home to Wales's first factory outlet shopping village, with a wide selection of goods including fashion, toys and ceramics.

Ebbw Vale and its surroundings are steeped in industrial history. Two unusual military-style round towers at nearby Nantyglo were built by ironmasters fearful of a workers' uprising. The great Welsh politician Aneurin Bevan (1897–1960) served as MP for Ebbw Vale (there is a monument to him just west of the town).

Places to visit

Ebbw Vale
Festival Park
Tel (01495) 350010 F
This park retains many of the original features of Garden Festival Wales 1992 and contains Wales's first factory outlet shopping village.

Festival Park, Ebbw Vale

Peaceful coast and country at Ferryside

Ferryside

Map Ref **C4**

Time, and traffic, seem to have passed Ferryside by – which doesn't bother the cockle-pickers along the estuary or the yachtsmen who use Ferryside as a peaceful sailing centre. The village stands in a charming backwater well off the main road and close to the junction of the Towy, Taf and Gwendraeth rivers. These three rivers form a fork-shaped waterway, bordered by sands, saltmarshes and green farmlands, as they flow into Carmarthen Bay.

There are magnificent views across the estuary from the minor road leading south from Ferryside, which clings to the hillside for the first mile. The rocky foreshore below the hill is the site of the vanished village of Hawton, destroyed in a huge storm about 300 years ago.

Pembrokeshire Coast
National Park

This is Britain's only coastal-based national park. It runs for about 180 miles from Amroth (near Tenby) in the south to St Dogmael's (near Cardigan) in the north, encompassing some of the most spectacular stretches of coastal natural beauty in Europe.

Although Pembrokeshire mainly conjures up images of cliffs and beaches, the national park boasts a tremendous variety of coastal scenery. The park can be divided into four parts. In the south, from Amroth to the mouth of the Milford Haven waterway, there are sandy beaches and towering limestone cliffs. The second part is the unexplored Daugleddau in the upper reaches of the Haven, where wooded creeks wind their way into the heart of Pembrokeshire.

The huge, horseshoe-shaped St Bride's Bay in the far west, fringed with more sea-cliffs and long stretches of sand, dominates the park's third part. Pembrokeshire at its most rugged is to be found in the final part of the park, the rock-bound north-facing shores between St David's and Cardigan. All in all, the park covers an area of some 225 square miles, rarely venturing inland for more than a few miles. The main exception to this general rule is to be found in the north, where the park's boundaries extend southwards to embrace the Preseli Hills, a moorland range rising to 536m (1760ft).

The best way to enjoy Pembrokeshire's scenic glories is on foot. The park authorities have made it easy for visitors by creating a footpath which runs almost all the way around the coast (the oil industry's installations along the Haven are the main interruption to this long-distance route). In walking this path you'll follow a shoreline rich in wildlife. Pembrokeshire is famous for its sea-bird populations – the razorbill is an appropriate symbol for a national park which is an ornithological paradise. The cliffs are a blaze of wild flowers which flourish in Pembrokeshire's balmy, mild climate, and seals can often be seen basking on the rocks below.

The national park organises an excellent series of guided walks. For further details on all aspects of the park call in at its information centres at Broad Haven, Haverfordwest, Newport, Pembroke, St David's and Tenby (see Tourist Information Centres on page 3).

Lower Fishguard's sheltered harbour

Fishguard/Goodwick Map Ref **B3**

Fishguard's Welsh name is Abergwaun, meaning 'mouth of the River Gwaun'. The prettiest part of Fishguard – known as the Lower Town or Lower Fishguard – is clustered around the old quayside where the Gwaun flows into the sea. Its row of gabled harbourside cottages, sheltering beneath a steep, gorse-covered headland, is wonderfully photogenic – a quality exploited by the makers of the 1971 film, starring Elizabeth Taylor and Richard Burton, of Dylan Thomas's *Under Milk Wood*, when Lower Fishguard became the imaginary, magical sea-town of Llareggub.

The main town of Upper Fishguard spreads itself out on the hill above the harbour. The Royal Oak Inn contains mementos of a little-known historic event – the last invasion of British soil. Its obscurity is probably a result of its remote location and the tragicomic nature of the episode. An ill-equipped French force, led by an Irish-American general, landed at nearby Carregwastad Point on 22 February 1797. The 'invasion' was a short-lived affair, the French surrendering without engaging in conflict. St Mary's Church has a tombstone to Jemima Nicholas, a formidable local character who captured 12 Frenchmen single handed, armed only with a pitchfork!

Fishguard's Market Hall contains items from the town's seafaring past, including records of lives saved by the local lifeboats. The modern port is a purpose-built harbour, created in the early 20th century at Goodwick just across the bay from Lower Fishguard. The A40 travels westwards across England and Wales to terminate at the quayside of this busy Irish Sea port, with ferry services to Rosslare.

To the west is rocky Strumble Head, its savage coastline marked by a lighthouse which stands on a little island linked to the mainland by a footbridge. In the lanes near St Nicholas is the Tregwynt Woollen Mill, a working mill open to the public which produces traditional and original Welsh weaves. Traditional methods can also be seen in use at the Llangloffan Farmhouse Cheese Centre, Castle Morris, where tasty Welsh cheese are handmade from the milk of the farm's own herd of cows.

Fishguard hosts a well-established Music Festival each summer which covers all types of music from jazz to orchestral.

Places to visit

Fishguard/Goodwick
Nearby
Llangloffan Farmhouse Cheese Centre, Castle Morris
Tel (01348) 891241 C
Morning demonstrations of the three stages of cheesemaking. Also stroll around the farm, see the animals.

Tregwynt Woollen Mill, nr St Nicholas
Tel (01348) 891225 F
Whitewashed mill in lovely spot dating from the 18th century.

Llangloffan Farmhouse Cheese Centre

Places to visit

Gelligaer

Llancaiach Fawr Manor
Tel (01443) 412248 C
Living history museum which
recaptures sights, sounds and smells of
Civil War period – Charles I actually
visited this Tudor mansion house, built
c.1530. Visitor centre, audio-visual
room, gardens.

Gelligaer

Map Ref **G5**

This unassuming valleys settlement hides its history too
well. Gelligaer was the site of a Roman fort, but you have
to look hard to find evidence of this. The only visible signs
are the undulations in a field in the centre of the village,
which represent all that's left of the fort's defensive ditches.
The field is fenced off, and next to it is a more recent
historical relic – the site of the first Lewis School, founded
in 1729 by a local benefactor. A roadside boulder with a
plaque marks the spot.

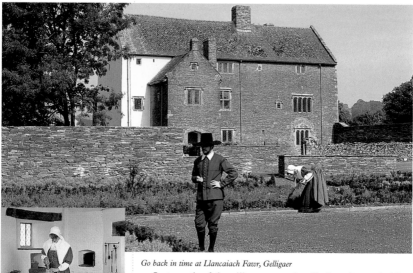

Go back in time at Llancaiach Fawr, Gelligaer

Just north of the village an unclassified road – probably
once part of the famous Roman highway known as Sarn
Helen – crosses Gelligaer Common, a bare but
atmospheric plateau where cairns and tumuli provide
evidence of ancient occupation. A short distance to the
west is Llancaiach Fawr Manor, a popular attraction.

Places to visit

Grosmont
Grosmont Castle F
An important border stronghold.

Grosmont

Map Ref **H3**

Grosmont, tucked away in a sleepy corner of the
borderlands, was not always so peaceful. Its castle was built
to command the border during the troublesome medieval
period. The Norman stronghold, originally an earthen
mound topped by timber defences, also gave
the village its name (the French *gros mont*
meaning 'big hill').

Grosmont Castle

The castle was later rebuilt in stone. As it
now stands, the fortress dates largely from the
early 13th century. Along with White Castle
and Skenfrith Castle, Grosmont is one of the
so-called 'Three Castles', a triangle of
fortresses which controlled the routes between
England and Wales on this strategically
important stretch of border country. The
village's Church of St Nicholas is a remarkable
size for such a small community, a
consequence of the presence of the castle and
the fact that Grosmont enjoyed borough status
until 1857.

Gwaun Valley

Map Ref **B3**

The residents of this secluded valley are quite happy to be behind the times. They still celebrate the New Year in the middle of January, based on the old calendar in use before 1752. They also have other reasons to feel distanced from the modern world. Their beautiful valley, clothed in ancient oakwoods, runs south-east from Fishguard into the unpopulated, untouched foothills of the Preselis.

Haverfordwest

Map Ref **B4**

Don't miss the opportunity to visit Haverfordwest if you are staying on the Pembrokeshire coast. This historic town of steep streets, riverside shops and handsome houses is crammed full of interest. For a bird's-eye view of everything, go first to the ruined 12th-century castle on the hill high above the rooftops. The strategic value of the site, above the western arm of the River Cleddau with panoramic views across the surrounding countryside, is plain to see. The stonework that has survived is exceptionally strong, defeating even the attempts made by Cromwell's men to demolish the castle during the Civil War. There's more history next door at Castle House, location of the town museum.

The riverside, Haverfordwest

Visitors to the museum might be surprised to discover that Haverfordwest was a thriving port from late medieval times. The Western Cleddau was once navigable all the way to the town, giving Haverfordwest access to the Milford Haven waterway and the open seas. Echoes of the town's sea-trading days remain along the Old Quay, a waterfront lined with warehouses and an inn whose name – the Bristol Trader – reflects the strong links that existed between Haverfordwest and the West Country.

The riverside has changed beyond recognition at the opposite end of town, where a marketplace and shops are part of an attractive waterfront development. Haverfordwest's true personality, though, remains rooted in the past. Imposing buildings and Georgian thoroughfares are reminders of Haverfordwest's historic role as Pembrokeshire's county town. Castle Square is surrounded by some of the town's most elegant architecture, and at the foot of the spacious High Street stands the old Shire Hall (now a court), with a fine neo-Classical façade.

St Mary's Church, at the top of the street, has wonderful stained glass windows and a splendid arcade of decoratively carved arches. On the opposite side of the street look out for the chamber, its entrance blocked by bars, sunk into the pavement. This strange medieval survivor was a crypt in which bones were stored from an overcrowded churchyard. Another medieval site, the ruined Haverfordwest Priory, is located beside the Cleddau at the end of the Old Quay.

Places to visit
Gwaun Valley
Penlan Uchaf Gardens
Tel (01348) 881388 C
Attractive landscaped surroundings with views of the Preseli Hills. Just over 1 hectare (3 acres).

Places to visit
Haverfordwest
Haverfordwest Castle F
Hilltop ruin above town. Superb views.

Haverfordwest Priory F
Ruins of old religious site, still under excavation.

Haverfordwest Town Museum
Tel (01437) 763087 C
Tells the story of the town from medieval to present times.

Nearby
Nant-y-Coy Mill, Treffgarne
Tel (01437) 741671 C **(voluntary)**
Mill wheel and grinding stones, 19th-century cottage, museum of local history, nature walk, craft workshops.

Pembrokeshire Motor Museum, Keeston Hill
Tel (01437) 710950 C
Collection of vintage, veteran and classic cars and motorcycles.

Picton Castle and Woodland Gardens, The Rhos
Tel (01437) 751326 C
The country house, a family home since 13th century, is open some afternoons. Beautiful gardens open on a more regular basis. Natural woodlands, shrubs, flowers, walled garden.

Scolton Manor and Country Park (off B4329)
Tel (01437) 731328 (House)/ 731457 (Park) C
Countryside centre, landscaped grounds, arboretum, woodlands, nature trail, railway exhibits. Authentically restored 19th-century manor house. Museum concentrates on telling story of Victorian life on a country estate.

Wiston Castle F
Remnants of fortification built on medieval 'Landsker' boundary between south and north Pembrokeshire.

The Old Bridge, Haverfordwest

Hay-on-Wye, the 'town of books'

Places to visit

Hay-on-Wye

Hay Castle
In private ownership. View from outside only.

Hay Crafts Centre F
Collection of stylish craft workshops – knitwear, glass, ceramics, leather, wood.

Nearby
Maesyronnen Chapel (off A438 between Glasbury and Llowes)
Wales's first chapel?

Hay Castle

Hay-on-Wye

Map Ref **G3**

Bibliophiles will need no introduction to this charming little borderland town. Over the years, Hay has earned an unlikely reputation for itself as the second-hand book capital of the world. There are bookshops everywhere – along the main street next to the grocery and baker's shops, tucked away in nooks and crannies around the old marketplace, even in a building which previously served as the town's cinema!

At the last count Hay-on-Wye boasted around 25 bookshops, specializing in everything from rare antiquarian volumes to new books. There are shops where serious collectors congregate; and there are general interest shops where you can spend a day browsing through thousands and thousands of titles hunting for second-hand bargains. Some shops specialize in military books, others in art, poetry and cookery titles, while the larger premises cover a comprehensive range of subjects. With such a strong bookish persona, it is not surprising that Hay now hosts an important Literature Festival in early summer each year which attracts a cast of internationally famous writers.

Standing on high ground above the streets is Hay Castle, originally Norman, but now a late-Tudor mansion, in private ownership and under restoration. The narrow streets below are full of attractive old buildings – look out in particular for the colonnaded open market and elegant Town Hall.

Not surprisingly, other shops have opened in Hay to take advantage of its regular flow of visitors. The town has interesting antiquarian print and art shops, and a modern, purpose-built crafts centre – featuring the work of a number of craftspeople – stands beside the main car park.

A spectacular mountain road south from Hay climbs to the 542m (1778ft) summit of the Gospel Pass in the Black Mountains before dropping down into the secluded Vale of Ewyas, Capel-y-ffin and Llanthony. It is very narrow in parts, and two-way traffic calls for extra caution during busy summer periods.

A few miles west of Hay, just off the A438, is Maesyronnen Chapel. Wales is a land of chapels, of which unassuming Maesyronnen is probably the first. The stone long house, built in about 1696 and still filled with wooden furniture from the 18th and 19th centuries, was originally a secret meeting place of Nonconformist dissenters. The churchyard at nearby Llowes contains a fine Celtic cross.

Kidwelly

Map Ref **D4**

Kidwelly is the home of one of South Wales's best-kept secrets. Its castle deserves much greater fame, for this medieval fortress is remarkably well preserved. The first sight of the castle is enough to tell visitors that this particular stronghold is something special. A soaring twin-towered three-storeyed gatehouse, standing to its full height, guards the entrance to a castle which dates from the early 12th century.

In the following centuries, Kidwelly was added to and remodelled to create the castle we see today. Purposeful and powerful, it occupies a steep ridge above the River Gwendraeth. The stronghold, defended by a series of round towers and concentric 'walls within walls', gives the impression of being the perfect stone castle – an image much sought after by film-makers, who have not been slow in using Kidwelly as the ideal medieval castle.

The castle precincts can be entered through a frail-looking town gate. Fragments of the fortified medieval town survive amongst Kidwelly's streets, which contain many old buildings.

The story of the town's recent past is told at the Kidwelly Industrial Museum. This was one of Britain's largest tinplate manufacturing centres in the 19th century. The museum, based at an old tinplate works, preserves the giant rolling mills, steam engines and sorting and boxing

Kidwelly Castle

rooms. The extensive site also contains a coal museum with exhibits – including pit head-gear – from local collieries.

To complete the story of Kidwelly, take the minor road south-west across the railway line to the refurbished Kidwelly Quay on the mouth of the Gwendraeth. Silence now reigns over the saltings and low-tide mudflats of a harbour that thrived during Kidwelly's days as a trading port.

Places to visit

Kidwelly
Kidwelly Castle
Tel (01554) 890104 C
Marvellously intact medieval fortress.

Kidwelly Industrial Museum
Tel (01554) 891078 C
Based at a tinplate works, founded in 1737, on outskirts of town.

Langland Bay

Map Ref **D5**

The sands of Langland Bay are just around rocky Mumbles Head. This popular south-facing Gower beach, close to Swansea, shelters between protective cliffs. A scenic cliff path leads westwards to neighbouring Caswell Bay. There is an attractively located golf course on the headland between the two bays.

Langland Bay

The Boathouse and (top)
Dylan Thomas's writing shed

Laugharne   Map Ref C4

No one has captured the atmosphere of this sleepy sea-town on the Taf Estuary better than its most famous resident, writer and poet Dylan Thomas. Laugharne was the 'timeless, mild, beguiling island of a town', the place where Dylan 'got off the bus and forgot to get on again'. He lived at The Boathouse, his 'house on stilts' by the swirling, silent, sea and sands of the estuary's 'heron-priested shore'.

The spirit of Laugharne, which mingled in his mind with memories of time spent at New Quay on Cardigan Bay, inspired the writing of his most famous work, *Under Milk Wood*. This 'play for voices' is a mesmerizing day in the life of a mythical Welsh coastal community called Llareggub (spell it backwards), populated by such characters as Captain Cat, Mrs Ogmore-Pritchard and Willy Nilly the postman.

Some of Dylan's happiest, most productive times were spent at Laugharne. He died in New York in 1953 and is buried in Laugharne's churchyard, his grave marked by a plain white cross. The Boathouse is now a museum dedicated to his life and work.

Laugharne Castle, standing beside the sea, is of medieval origin with Tudor additions. Excavations have revealed evidence of a historic site which served as a comfortable mansion as well as military stronghold. Its elaborate Georgian and Victorian garden is being recreated.

Places to visit

Laugharne

Dylan Thomas Boathouse
Tel (01994) 427420 C
Original writings and furnishings, audio-visual presentation. Nearby is his cramped writing shed.

Laugharne Castle
Tel (01994) 427906 C
Picturesque castle overlooking the Taf Estuary.

Places to visit

Lawrenny
Nearby
Cwm Deri Vineyard, Martletwy
Tel (01834) 891274 F
Self-guided vineyard walk, exhibition, animals, picnic area.

Lawrenny   Map Ref B4

Many visitors approach Lawrenny by sea, for the quayside here is a popular sailing centre. The quay stands at the meeting place of the Cresswell and Carew rivers and the larger Daugleddau river system on the upper reaches of the Milford Haven waterway. Sailing on these waters is superb: the wooded, sheltered banks of the Daugleddau and its tributaries wind their way deep into the heart of Pembrokeshire, but also allow access to the open seas.

The village of Lawrenny itself is almost a mile from the quay. It is dominated by the tall, four-storeyed tower of St Caradog's Church. The tower, a fine example of the local style, has been described as 'in effect and proportion one of the noblest of its type'. To the east is Cresswell, a pretty village beside wooded riverbanks.

Llandeilo

Map Ref **D4**

Llandeilo sits contentedly on a bosky rise above the rich farmlands of the Towy Valley. Its slender 111m (365ft) arched bridge across the Towy is reputedly the longest single-span stone bridge in Wales. From here, the road climbs up to the Church of St Teilo and the town's narrow main shopping street.

There are some beautiful woodlands around and about. Some of the finest belong to Dinefwr Park, a wonderful National Trust landscape laid out by Capability Brown in the 18th century. The sweeping grounds, ranged around Newton House, contain White Park cattle, an extremely rare breed that has been associated with Dinefwr Park for over 900 years. Dinefwr was an influential seat of power in medieval times as the home of the native Welsh leader Lord Rhys, 'Prince of South Wales'. The romantic ruin of Dinefwr Castle stands on a wooded cliff above the river and the Castle Woods Nature Reserve, a 25-hectare (62-acre) sanctuary based around the south and west slopes of the castle. There is access to the castle from Dinefwr Park, though the site is not fully open to the public.

The hills south-east of Llandeilo are a hideaway for one of Wales's most memorable castles. The gnarled ruins of Carreg Cennen Castle occupy a breathtaking location on the edge of a sheer-sided limestone cliff overlooking the brooding Black Mountain. Carreg Cennen's weather-beaten, time-worn masonry evokes an authentic medieval atmosphere, and also due respect for any would-be attackers: during the stiff climb to the summit, visitors have plenty of time to contemplate the daunting prospect the castle must have presented to assault forces.

Tumbledown Dryslwyn Castle, on its sizeable tump west of Llandeilo, really looks its age. The stronghold was built by native Welsh leaders to control a crossing point on the Towy. Sections of wall survive from a substantial stronghold which included a medieval township. On the valley's southern ridge overlooking Dryslwyn is Paxton's Tower, a memorial to Lord Nelson put up in the early 19th century by local landowner Sir William Paxton (see Carmarthen entry).

This side of the valley is also the home of the beautiful Gelli Aur Country Park, a 36-hectare (90-acre) swathe of wooded parkland surrounding a magnificent mansion. Gelli Aur (the 'Golden Grove') has splendid views across the valley from the terrace gardens, an arboretum, nature trails and deer park.

Carreg Cennen Castle, near Llandeilo

Places to visit

Llandeilo
Dinefwr Castle
Ruin romantically perched on cliff on outskirts of town. Site not fully open to the public due to restoration work.

Dinefwr Park 🦌
Tel (01558) 823902 C
Expansive 18th-century landscaped park, famous Dinefwr White Park cattle, ancient deer park, bog wood and boardwalk walkway, restored Victorian garden. Limited access also to Newton House, a 17th-century building with Victorian Gothic façade.

Nearby
Carreg Cennen Castle, Trapp
Tel (01558) 822291 C
13th-century castle in dramatic location. Walled passageway in cliff leads to cave beneath castle. Castle approached through a Welsh hill farm with 17th-century longhouse, rare breeds and farm animals.

Dryslwyn Castle F
Prominent ruin 5 miles west of Llandeilo. Limited access due to conservation work.

Gelli Aur Country Park (off B4300 west of Llandeilo)
Tel (01558) 668885 F
Visitor centre, guided walks, craft demonstrations, beautiful setting.

Llyn Llech Owain Country Park (off A476 just north of Cross Hands)
Tel (01269) 832229 F
63-hectare (156-acre) park based around lake with woodland, footpaths, cycle trails, visitor centre.

Llyn Llech Owain Country Park

Llandovery

Map Ref **E3**

The River Towy rushes through a rocky gorge north of Llandovery

George Borrow, in his classic 19th-century travel book *Wild Wales,* called Llandovery 'the pleasantest little town in which I have halted'. He would have little cause to revise his description if he visited the Llandovery of today, for nothing of substance has changed since his times. Llandovery's cobbled market square, archways, clock tower and Georgian façades retain a period charm. The old inns and hostelries have an unpretentious, typically rural Welsh appearance. And the castle, a stumpy, unrestored ruin just off the main street, remains standing – but only just.

The hilltop which guards the north-eastern approach to the town, once the site of a Roman fort, is occupied by a large church with a lofty, buttressed 13th-century square tower. Llandovery is the home of Wales's only Welsh-speaking public school.

Places to visit

Llandovery

Dinefwr Crafts Centre
Tel (01550) 721452 F
Variety of craft shops under one roof.

Llandovery Heritage Centre
Tel (01550) 721228 C
Celebrates history and legends of the area. In attractively restored Georgian building above Tourist Information Centre.

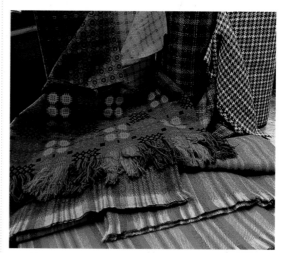

The tradition of weaving lives on in rural Wales

Places to visit

Llandysul

Nearby
Rock Mills (Y Felin Wlan),
Capel Dewi (off B4459)
Tel (01559) 362356 C
Family-run firm founded a century ago, with working waterwheel driven by River Clettwr. Products on sale in the craft shop. Appealing down-to-earth atmosphere.

Llandysul

Map Ref **D3**

Llandysul has the air of a town still rooted in its old country ways. Its long main shopping street has a quiet dignity and pleasing variety, scarcely any two buildings being alike. Note the squat, no-nonsense look of Ebenezer Chapel, built in 1833. The offices of the Gomer Press, long-established Welsh publishers, are on the opposite side of the street.

Running parallel, at a lower level, is the road providing access to St Tysul's Church. This is well worth a visit for the beauty of its interior. Built in Early English style, it has massive square pillars with pointed arches. There are some flowery inscriptions to the local gentry of bygone days and an ancient altar stone with incised Christian markings in the Lady Chapel.

The church has had secular as well as religious uses. Two centuries ago the porch served as one of the goals for a no-holds-barred annual football match. The old Welsh game of 'chware pel' was played around the church tower and a sexton of the early 18th century claimed to be able to throw the ball right over the top.

Llandysul is in an area that once abounded with woollen mills, some of which remain to keep the tradition alive. The Teifi rushes through a rocky, narrow course at Llandysul, attracting canoeists and slalom competitors to its challenging waters. The Castell Howell Family Club at Pont-siân north of the town as a range of leisure facilities, including pool, sauna and squash. Gŵyl Werin y Cnapan, Europe's largest Celtic folk festival, is staged each July at nearby Ffostrasol.

Town Hall, Llanelli

Llanelli

Map Ref **D5**

There's more to Llanelli than first meets the eye. The town is graced with attractive parklands and – surprise, surprise – a delightful little sandy beach. To find the beach, you head westwards from the town centre to the old docklands. There, fronting the now silent North Docks, is a pretty stretch of sands with superb views over the bay to the north coast of the Gower Peninsula.

Llanelli's People's Park, behind a highly decorative Town Hall, is only a short walk from the pedestrianized shopping centre. Parc Howard, on the hill above, has large areas of grassland, a rose garden, and a Victorian Mansion House which contains a museum with displays on two products for which Llanelli was once famous – pottery and tinplate.

Rugby enthusiasts gather at Llanelli's Stradey Park, home of the celebrated 'Scarlets', the Llanelli Rugby Club, leading exponents of Wales's national sport. Look out for the sospans (saucepans) on the rugby posts, a reminder of Llanelli's metal-producing past and inspiration for the rousing local anthem, 'Sospan Fach' (The Little Saucepan).

Wildfowl and Wetlands Centre, near Llanelli

The River Loughor meets the sea along Llanelli's shores in a wide estuary of sand and saltmarsh. A stretch just south-east of the town has been developed as an important wildfowl reserve based on the highly successful 'Slimbridge' concept. The old steelworks site west of the town centre has been completely transformed into an attractive area of grassland and water. Further large-scale waterfront redevelopment is taking place as part of the multi-million pound Millennium Coastal Park scheme, an imaginative refurbishment of an 8-mile coastal strip between Loughor Bridge and Pembrey involving landscaping, new leisure facilities, footpaths and cycleways. The scheme is scheduled for completion in 2000.

In the hills to the north is the Cwm Lleidi Country Park, based around a reservoir in a wooded area known locally as Swiss Valley. The sands and forests of the Pembrey Country Park are also close by (see Pembrey entry).

Places to visit

Llanelli
Parc Howard Mansion Museum
Tel (01554) 773538 F
Local exhibits and art gallery.

Nearby
Cwm Lleidi Country Park (about 2 miles north of town centre) F
Lakeside walks, fishing.

Wildfowl and Wetlands Centre (on estuary 2 miles south-east of Llanelli)
Tel (01554) 741087 C
Located at Wales's premier estuary for wildfowl and waders. Visitor centre, observations points.

Places to visit

Llangadog

Nearby

Garn Goch F

Massive stone ramparts still survive of an Iron Age hillfort.

Llangadog

Map Ref **E3**

This traditional Welsh village and market centre stands slightly above the River Towy on the approach to the brooding Black Mountain, a bleakly beautiful upland mass in the western corner of the Brecon Beacons National Park. The A4069 south of Llangadog winds its way in scenic loops over the mountain. Stop at the north-facing car park below Foel Fawr and enjoy the wonderful panoramas. The road then rises to nearly 500m (over 1600ft) before dropping down to Brynaman.

The tree-covered mound on private land which can be seen from the roadside $^1/_2$ mile south of Llangadog is the remains of an early motte-and-bailey castle put up by the Normans. A much older – and much more impressive – historic site stands in wild countryside a few miles to the south-west. This is Garn Goch, a remarkable Iron Age hillfort, one of the largest in Wales, with massive fortifications. The easiest way to approach Garn Goch is through Bethlehem, a hamlet famous for its Christmas postmark.

Llangadog stands in the foothills of the Black Mountain

Llangorse

Map Ref **G3**

The village of Llangorse has grown up close to Llangorse Lake, the largest natural lake in South Wales. Llangorse village stands a short distance from the lakeside. Its centrepiece is an ancient church with pre-medieval roots, on a religious site founded in about the 6th century by St Paulinus, tutor to St David, Wales's patron saint. A Viking burial stone has been uncovered here.

Most visitors approach Llangorse Lake from the north, crossing the grassy common to the lakeside which has become a popular watersports centre. The reedy banks and $1^1/_2$-mile-long waters are also a popular habitat for birds and an important wildlife site, though birdwatching and some water-based activities are sometimes incompatible. Legend has it that the lake covers an ancient city. We know for certain that Llangorse was once settled by lake-dwellers – their small artificial island can still be seen from the shore.

Llangorse Lake

Llangorse's peaceful lakesides lie on its southern shores, around Llangasty Talyllyn's interesting 19th-century church. The area abounds with pony trekking and activity centres, including an indoor climbing centre.

Llansteffan

Map Ref C4

Llansteffan Castle looks down from its headland perch over tranquil coast and countryside. The village lies below, alongside the sandy mouth of the River Towy. The castle occupies a commanding position that has been defended since prehistoric times. Its rough stone walls, dating from 1192, enclose a much earlier site – an Iron Age promontory fort occupied in 600BC. Llansteffan's massive twin-towered gatehouse still has the power to intimidate, though the most outstanding feature of this site is the huge view across Carmarthen Bay to the western tip of the Gower Peninsula.

Llansteffan Castle

Llanthony

Map Ref G3

Mountain-locked Llanthony was 'truly calculated for religion and more adapted to the canonical discipline than all the monasteries of the British Isles'. These were the words used to describe Llanthony Priory by the medieval traveller and chronicler Giraldus Cambrensis, Gerald of Wales.

Religious men seeking solitude and austerity must have found the ideal spot at Llanthony. They first came in the 6th century, building a chapel to St David. This ruined chapel was discovered in the 12th century by the Norman knight William de Lacy. Renouncing all worldly pursuits, he established a hermitage here which subsequently became a priory. Although now an 800-year-old ruin, the original beauty of the building and its setting can still be evoked, especially since so little of the surrounding countryside has changed. Llanthony's former magnificence lives on in its surviving richly decorated red stonework and quite superb row of pointed Early English archways.

The 19th-century poet Walter Savage Landor was another person to be captivated by the compelling beauty of the place. His love affair was short-lived. He soon became disenchanted with the 'wretched Welsh' – who were equally as disenchanted with their miscast lord of the manor – and he left under a cloud in 1813, never to return.

The priory's car park is a good starting point for walks along the borderland Offa's Dyke Path. Llanthony also stands amidst some of the Black Mountains' best pony trekking country. The narrow road to the north passes Capel-y-ffin (and the ruins of the confusingly named Llanthony Monastery) before climbing up the spectacular Gospel Pass. To the south, enthusiasts of odd religious architecture should not miss Cwmyoy's tipsy church, whose wonky tower and leaning walls are victims of subsidence.

Llanthony Priory

A Look at
Welsh History

South Wales has seen it all – prehistoric man, Roman invaders, early religious leaders, medieval warlords and the Industrial Revolution. The tides of history have left a legacy of sites and monuments linking the mists of time with the 19th century.

At the one end of the spectrum there are prehistoric stone tombs such as the Pentre Ifan Cromlech near Newport in north Pembrokeshire, and St Lythans and Tinkinswood near Barry in the Vale of Glamorgan. Iron Age man built countless hillforts for security, the largest of which is Garn Goch in the foothills of the Black Mountain near Llangadog.

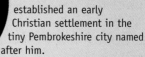

Then came the Romans. The importance of their base at Caerleon is not generally appreciated. The town, Isca to the Romans, was one of only three bases in Britain built to accommodate their crack legionary troops. Much evidence remains of their stay, including a magnificent amphitheatre. Deep in the hills at Pumsaint is another important Roman site – the only place in Britain where we know, for definite, that they mined for gold.

The Age of Saints produced some remarkable men. In the 6th century, St Illtud founded a monastic community at Llantwit Major. Shortly afterwards, St David, Wales's patron saint, established an early Christian settlement in the tiny Pembrokeshire city named after him.

Wales is renowned as a land of castles. The Normans arrived in strength from the 11th century onwards, building castles as they pushed further west. Their strongholds still stand today, powerful monuments of a troubled time in Welsh history. At Caerphilly, for example, they built one of Europe's greatest medieval fortresses, whose massive stone and water defences still intimidate the onlooker.

Other mighty symbols of a belligerent age in South Wales include castles at Pembroke and Kidwelly. But medieval times also saw the establishment of peaceful religious sites such as Tintern Abbey and remote Llanthony Priory.

Industrialization was the final historic force which had a profound effect here. In the 18th and 19th centuries, the South Wales Valleys produced vast quantities of coal, iron and steel. Heavy industry has all but disappeared now, though the old days are remembered at such sites as Blaenafon's Big Pit Mining Museum and the Rhondda Heritage Park.

Llantilio Crossenny

Map Ref **H4**

Pleasantly located Llantilio Crossenny stands deep in rolling border country. The peaceful fields and farmlands around the village were strategically important to medieval military men. In the lanes to the north-west is White Castle, one of the 'Three Castles' (the other two are at Grosmont and Skenfrith) built to control the border.

White Castle still looks the part. Formidable round towers and stout curtain walls surmount a grassy mound which is encircled by a deep, water-filled moat. The only addition needed to complete the scene is the white plaster rendering that originally covered the masonry, giving the castle its name.

Nearer the village a rectangular moat marks the site of Hen Gwrt (Old Court) on which a palace of the Bishops of Llandaff once stood.

Places to visit

Llantilio Crossenny
Nearby
White Castle
(1½ miles north-west of village)
Tel (01600) 780380 C
Moated fortress, one of the Welsh border's famous 'Three Castles'.

Inside White Castle

Llantrisant

Map Ref **F5**

Llantrisant is a quaint hilltop town with an intriguing history. It had its first charter in 1346 and provided warriors for the Black Prince in the French wars of the 14th century. Late in Victorian times it came into prominence again when a local doctor, William Price, a life-long rebel, cremated his infant son Iesu Grist (Jesus Christ) on an open-air pyre. There was a public outcry but cremation was legalized as a result. A statue to the redoubtable doctor – an incredible character who also believed in vegetarianism, nudism, free love and radical politics – stands in the Bull Ring.

To reach the old town proper, turn up the steep S-bend off the A473 between Talbot Green and Tonteg. There are extensive views across the Vale of Glamorgan from the parish church on the crest of the hill.

Since the mid-1970s the town has been the home of the Royal Mint, which is sited in a business park beyond Llantrisant Common.

Places to visit

Llantrisant
Llantrisant Castle F
Scanty ivy-covered remains of 13th-century castle, beyond open space near the Town Hall.

Model House Craft and Design Centre
Tel (01443) 237758 F
Attractive visitor centre where craftspeople can be seen at work. Changing exhibitions of high standard. Unique Royal Mint exhibition with historic machinery and replicas of old coins.

Llantwit Major

Map Ref **F6**

You could be forgiven for thinking that you are in a cathedral when you wander around Llantwit Major's vast church. Notwithstanding its size, the church has a pedigree that in many ways justifies cathedral status, for this was the site of the first Christian college in Britain.

Places to visit

Llantwit Major
St Illtud's Church (and collection of Celtic crosses)
Unusually large and imposing church. Important historic site.

Nearby
St Donat's Castle
Tel (01446) 792271 C
Guided tours for limited summer period. Castle dates from around 1300 but much restored in 20th century. Bought in 1925 by American newspaper tycoon William Randolph Hearst. Now the home of Atlantic College, the world's first international 6th-form school. St Donat's Arts Centre (exhibitions, theatre, etc) located at castle.

Llantwit Major is close to the spectacular Glamorgan Heritage Coast

Coracle fishermen can still be seen on the waters of the River Teifi

Llantwit Major is an anglicization of the Welsh Llanilltud Fawr, meaning 'the great church of Illtud'. St Illtud was an influential early Celtic teacher whose pupils, according to legend, included St David and St Patrick. The present church stands hidden in a hollow on or near the original monastic settlement. Anyone who has visited St David's Cathedral in the far south-west of Wales will be struck by the uncanny similarity in the siting of both buildings. The church, which dates from Norman times, houses a magnificent collection of Celtic crosses and inscribed stones.

Llantwit Major's mainly rocky beach lies 1 mile to the south in a break in the cliff-backed Glamorgan Heritage Coast. Further west is Nash Point, with fine views from the clifftop car park.

Llechryd
Map Ref C3

This idyllic spot in the Teifi Valley is a favourite haunt of salmon fishermen. The river flows beneath an ancient five-arch stone bridge, a good place to take the advice of poet W H Davies and 'stand and stare' as long as you can.

Llyn y Fan Fach/ Llyn y Fan Fawr
Map Ref E4

These remote mountain lakes were scooped out by glaciers in the last Ice Age. Even today, it is still possible to evoke something of the chilling desolation of a landscape bruised by savage conditions when you venture up to these lakes, high in the Black Mountain.

The best approach is from the hamlet of Llanddeusant. Walk up the unsurfaced track to the first – and smaller – of these lakes, Llyn y Fan Fach. Llyn y Fan Fach has its 'Lady of the Lake' legend. A magical lady rose from its waters and married a local farmer. If ever he struck her three times, she vowed to return to the lake. When the inevitable happened, she disappeared into its dark waters, taking all the farm animals with her. The legend is particularly interesting because of the possible connections between the lady's magic healing powers and the Physicians of Myddfai (see Myddfai entry).

Amphitheatre-like cliffs rise directly above Llyn y Fan Fach's waters to a sharp ridge leading to Fan Brycheiniog, at 802m (2630ft) the highest point in the Black Mountain. The larger lake, Llyn y Fan Fawr (fawr meaning 'big'), lies beneath the screes and severe escarpments of Fan Brycheiniog. A word of caution: while the walk to Llyn y Fan Fach is not demanding, it is unwise to climb into the inhospitable Black Mountain above unless you are experienced and well equipped.

Remote Llyn y Fan Fawr

Llysyfran

Map Ref **B4**

The Llysyfran Country Park, in farmlands 7 miles north-east of Haverfordwest, is based around the reservoir of the same name. Park and reservoir offer a wide range of recreational facilities, including sailing, canoeing, windsurfing and fishing. Walkers can follow a 7½-mile perimeter path around the wooded 76-hectare (187-acre) lake, which, as the only large area of lowland water in the region, has become a haven for wildlife.

Four miles to the east, on the minor road between Maenclochog and Llan-y-cefn (it's the country lane to the east of the B4313), is Penrhos Cottage. This small thatched dwelling was, according to local tradition, a Tŷ un nos (overnight house), built in one night between sunset and sunrise on common land.

Places to visit

Llysyfran
Llysyfran Country Park
Tel (01437) 532273 F
Offers water-based and country pursuits.

Nearby
Penrhos Cottage, nr Maenclochog
Tel Scolton House and Museum
(01437) 731328 for further
information C
Traditional Welsh cottage with period furniture.

Wallis Woollen Mill, Ambleston
Tel (01437) 731297 F
19th-century mill weaving own range of fabrics in pure wool.

Llysyfran Country Park

Loughor

Map Ref **D5**

The ruined castle by the bridge on the western end of town was built on the site of a Roman fort in Norman times. The ruins stand above what was once a low-tide fording point across the Loughor Estuary. The castle's most conspicuous remnant is its single surviving tower.

Places to visit

Loughor 🅿
Loughor Castle F
Scant remains.

Maesteg

Map Ref **E5**

Maesteg, near the head of the Llynfi Valley, is almost enclosed by high, forested slopes. One of the most imposing edifices in this former coalmining town is the Town Hall, its tall clock tower overlooking the central square. The hall, used for exhibitions and entertainments, gave actor Richard Burton, born in nearby Pont-rhydyfen, his first chance to appear on stage. The daily market beneath the hall is at its biggest and busiest on Fridays, when it spills out into the surrounding area. Maesteg's sports centre is based around another noteworthy building – an imaginatively refurbished and converted blast furnace engine house.

Llangynwyd in the hills to the south is one of the pretty villages around and about which still retain their rural charm. Its thatched inn, next to a tall-towered church, is one of the oldest in Wales. Around the New Year period, the village is the scene of the traditional Mari Lwyd (Grey Mare) celebrations.

The estuary at Loughor

Manorbier Castle

Places to visit

Manorbier
Manorbier Castle
Tel (01834) 871394 C
Unusually intact picture of a Norman
baronial residence, with gardens,
chapel, state apartments, etc.

Manorbier   Map Ref **B5**

In the history books, Manorbier is linked with the
description 'the most delightful part of Pembroke ... the
pleasantest spot in Wales'. These words were coined by
Giraldus Cambrensis (Gerald of Wales), a medieval
religious man, traveller and chronicler. Giraldus was hardly
impartial in the matter, for he was born, in 1146, at
Manorbier Castle. But it would be churlish to dispute his
description, since Manorbier remains undisputedly a pretty
place.

    Giraldus was a major figure in medieval Wales, a
churchman of Norman stock who wrote widely about
Wales and the native Welsh. His birthplace, a notably well-
preserved fortification, stands on a rise overlooking a
delightfully unspoilt sandy bay.

Marloes   Map Ref **A4**

The remote village of Marloes is lucky enough to be near
to one of Wales's most beautiful beaches. Marloes Sands,
below an amphitheatre of red-tinged cliffs, stretch for
about $3/4$ of a mile between two headlands. The beach, of
firm golden sands pierced by weirdly shaped rocky
outcrops, is accessible by footpath from a car park about
1 mile west of the village.

    Guarding the beach's western approach is Gateholm, a
narrow island accessible at low tide, which contains
evidence of an ancient Romano-British settlement. The
'top' road west from Marloes goes as far as Martin's
Haven, a rocky inlet at the approach to Deer Park, a
rugged peninsula which contains an Iron Age promontory
fort and some exceptional coastal scenery. Martin's Haven
is the embarkation point for seasonal boat trips to Skomer
Island, a short distance offshore (there are also much less
frequent trips to Skokholm and Grassholm islands).

The beach at Marloes

Merthyr Mawr   Map Ref **F5**

The dune system of the Merthyr Mawr Warren is a mini-
desert. Tall, grassy dunes, some of the largest in Europe,
cover a wide area between Porthcawl and the mouth of the
River Ogmore. This strange, shifting landscape can be
explored by following a network of paths through the
dunes.

    The village of Merthyr Mawr stands at the eastern
approach to the warren. Its church, green fields and rustic
thatched cottages with their neat gardens create a picture
which is more characteristic of rural England than Wales.
Follow the road westwards from the village to Candleston
Castle, a sad and scanty ruin on the edge of the dunes.

Merthyr Tydfil

Map Ref F4

The old 'iron and steel capital of the world' is a more sedate town today than in its rip-roaring heyday during the Industrial Revolution. In those days Merthyr's night skies glowed bright as round-the-clock blast furnaces smelted metal which was used in railway lines as far afield as Siberia.

The town's volatile history comes as no surprise. Merthyr was ruled by the all-powerful ironmasters, whose workers were crammed together in tightly packed terraced communities. The 'us and them' nature of the town can be understood by comparing two of the surviving sites open to the public.

On the one hand, there's Cyfarthfa Castle, the imposing 19th-century home of the Crawshay ironmasters. This Gothic mansion stands in a landscaped 65-hectare (160-acre) parkland overlooking a part of Merthyr that contains Chapel Row, a preserved row of cramped workers' cottages, one of which – number 4 – was the birthplace (in 1841) of composer Dr Joseph Parry, writer of 'Myfanwy', a favourite tune much-performed by male-voice choirs. The stark contrast between privilege and poverty produced a politically conscious populace, and in 1900 Merthyr became the first town in Britain to elect a Socialist MP – Keir Hardie – to Parliament.

Another Merthyr 'first' was its pioneering railway. Contrary to popular belief, the world's first steam engine, invented by Cornishman Richard Trevithick, ran from

The Brecon Mountain Railway runs north from Merthyr Tydfil

Merthyr to Abercynon in 1804, beating Stephenson's *Rocket* by a full 20 years.

A monument to this feat stands at the top of the High Street. Other reminders of old Merthyr include the Ynysfach Iron Heritage Centre, an interpretive centre for the iron and steel industry located in a beautifully restored stone engine house, and the Dowlais Stables, an unexpectedly elegant Georgian-fronted structure where the horses for the nearby ironworks were kept.

Modern Merthyr is a busy shopping and commercial centre for the northern valleys. It stands at the meeting place between industrial and rural South Wales – the boundary of the Brecon Beacons National Park is only a five-minute drive from the town centre.

Places to visit

Merthyr Tydfil

Brecon Mountain Railway, Pant
Tel (01685) 722988. C
Narrow-gauge engines on a scenic 3½-mile route. One of the 'Great Little Trains of Wales'.

Cyfarthfa Castle Museum and Art Gallery
Tel (01685) 723112 C
Housed in authentic Regency surroundings. Extensive fine and decorative art collections. Social and industrial history is interpreted in atmospheric basements. Café Bardi within the museum is an Italian-style café, a homage to the South Wales Valleys' Italian communities.

Joseph Parry's Cottage,
4 Chapel Row
Tel (01685) 383704 F
Recreates the atmosphere of the 1840s.

Ynysfach Iron Heritage Centre
Tel (01685) 721858 C
1801 engine house with iron and steel displays.

Nearby
Garwnant Visitor Centre (off A470
5 miles north-west of town centre)
Tel (01685) 723060 F
Visitor centre in forest and lakeland setting with exhibitions, organized activities, walks, children's play area, picnic sites, mountain bike hire.

Preserved cottages at Chapel Row

A string of lakes, forests, open hillsides and pretty villages such as Pontsticill occupy the unspoilt countryside north of the town. The Brecon Mountain Railway runs from its terminus at Pant to a beautiful lakeside in the foothills of the Brecon Beacons. The site of Morlais Castle (in the hills near the terminus) commands fine views looking northwards. There is little to see of the tumbledown Norman ruin itself, save for a subterranean vaulted basement.

Milford Haven {Map Ref A4}

Milford Haven stands on the waterway of the same name considered by many – including Admiral Lord Nelson – to be one of the finest natural harbours in the world. The town, on a hillside above the shores, was created virtually as a 'new town' in the late 18th century, which accounts for its orderly 'grid-iron' street pattern. In its early days, it failed in its bid to lure the lucrative trans-Atlantic trade away from Liverpool and London. Milford had to wait until the mid- and late 19th century and the coming of the railways, docks and fishing industry before it began to fulfil its early promise.

The Friends' Meeting House of 1811 is a reminder of the town's links with the Quaker whaling families who settled here from Nantucket. The story of the town's seafaring past is told at the Milford Haven Museum in the refurbished docks. Major efforts have been made to attract new life to the docks, which now contain a 150-berth marina, dockside gallery, go-kart track, historic ships, adventure playground, Kaleidoscope Discovery Centre and visitor information centre.

For a splendid view across the town and waterway (and its supertanker berths and oil and petro-chemical installations), take a stroll along The Rath, an elevated road lined with pretty gardens.

The town's Meads Sports and Leisure Centre has excellent facilities, including indoor swimming pool, sauna and indoor bowls. The Torch Theatre, with its wide range of productions, is popular with locals and visitors alike.

Monmouth {Map Ref H4}

History buffs will have a field day at Monmouth. This prosperous border market town manages to give the impression that almost every one of its streets contains something of historic note. The best starting point for a town tour is Agincourt Square. Tall buildings and old inns surround this busy town-centre square, which is dominated by the grand façade of the early 18th-century Shire Hall. The statue beneath its clock face accounts for the square's name: it is of Henry V, winner of the famous battle at Agincourt in 1415.

Henry, who was born at Monmouth Castle in 1387, gazes down on to a statue of the town's second famous son, Charles Stewart Rolls, co-founder of Rolls-Royce. Rolls is depicted holding a model of the precarious-looking biplane in which he made the first non-stop flight to France and back (he died in an aviation accident in 1910).

The ruins of Monmouth Castle stand on a peaceful rise above the River Monnow only a stone's throw from the bustling square. The castle's bare, grey-stoned shell contrasts with the elaborate red-stoned frontage of Great

Places to visit

Milford Haven

Kaleidoscope Discovery Centre
Tel (01646) 695374 C
'Hands on' science discovery centre.

Milford Haven Museum
Tel (01646) 694496 C
Exhibits in old building originally used for storing whale oil.

The Milford Haven waterway attracts boats large and small

Places to visit

Monmouth

Castle and Regimental Museum
Tel (01600) 772175 F
Military history from Roman times and evolution of Royal Monmouthshire Royal Engineers.

Monmouth Castle F
Scant remains of Henry V's birthplace. View from outside only.

Monnow Bridge F
Fortified medieval bridge, a rare survivor.

Nelson Museum and Local History Centre
Tel (01600) 713519 C
Attractive museum with Nelson and Charles Rolls memorabilia.

Castle House opposite, built here in 1673 by a local nobleman so that his daughter-in-law could bear her first child 'near the spot of ground ... where our great hero Henry the Fifth was born.' Next door is the Castle and Regimental Museum which traces the military history of Monmouth.

Monmouth's most celebrated historic building stands at the far end of Monnow Street, guarding the western approach to the town. This the Monnow Bridge, a fortified gateway on a bridge across the river. Reputedly the only one of its kind in Britain, this gate, dating from the late 13th century, was built as an outer defence of the castle. It still serves something of its original purpose, as frustrated motorists queuing to squeeze through its narrow portal will testify.

There is a wealth of Georgian architecture to be seen throughout the town – look out, for example, for eye-catching Cornwall House along Monnow Street. As its name implies, the Nelson Museum and Local History Centre combines two themes – Admiral Lord Nelson and the story of this ancient market town. The comprehensive Nelson collection, which includes his fighting sword and the battle plans for Trafalgar, was given to the museum by Lady Llangattock, mother of Charles Rolls. Along the street from the museum is an elaborately decorated window (in a building which now serves as a Youth Hostel) dedicated to Geoffrey of Monmouth, a 12th-century cleric whose fanciful writings on the history of Britain became the source of many legends.

The Kymin, a 256m (840ft) hill overlooking the town, is crowned by a late 18th-century pavilion known as the Round House, and a Naval Temple, opened in 1801, which commemorates Britain's victories at sea.

Monmouth's Monnow Bridge and (above) Charles Rolls and Henry V at Agincourt Square

Monmouthshire and Brecon Canal

Map Ref **G4**

This tranquil waterway runs for 35 miles between Brecon and Pontypool. Originally, the waterway connected Brecon with Newport on the Severn Estuary, and transported everything from coal to fertilizer. Canal cruisers, canoeists and holiday craft now sail along its waters, past abandoned limekilns, old wharves and pretty villages – such as Talybont – well endowed with canalside inns.

Much of the waterway lies within the Brecon Beacons National Park. Here, the canal meanders along wooded hillsides on the shoulder of the lovely Usk Valley. You don't have to cruise the waters to enjoy the canal; many visitors now walk along part or all of its towpath. The area around Gilwern and Llanfoist is a good centre for canal cruiser hire. Boat trips operate from the Brecon end of the canal. For further information on the canal, please telephone (01873) 830328.

The canal near Llanfrynach

What to Do
on a Rainy Day

Yes, it does sometime rain in Wales. But don't worry, there are plenty of wet-weather attractions and places to visit to keep you – and the children – entertained. In Cardiff and Swansea, for example, you can take the kids swimming or tenpin bowling. Cardiff also has a superb ice rink and popular Techniquest science discovery centre, while you can forget all about the grey skies outside from within Swansea's Plantasia, which has desert and tropical climates controlled by computer.

You're transported into another world within Cardiff Castle, whose opulent interior is a dazzling example of money-no-object, over-the-top Victorian design. And you can spend an entire day wandering through the galleries of the National Museum at Cardiff's Civic Centre. At nearby Newport, take a tour of Tredegar House, one of Wales's finest mansions, a glittering residence which also shows visitors the 'downstairs' life of the servants' quarters.

The weather is irrelevant when you're underground. The highlight of a visit to the Big Pit Mining Museum at Blaenafon is the underground tour. You're kitted out with a safety hat and lamp before descending 91m (300ft) by pit cage for a tour of the old mineworkings conducted by ex-colliers. There's a totally different underground experience at the Dan-yr-Ogof Caves, Craig-y-nos. This is Europe's largest showcaves complex with three separate cave systems open to the public.

There's lots to see and do indoors at Folly Farm near Saundersfoot, a large working dairy farm open to the public with milking demonstrations and children's attractions. Although you're almost surrounded by water you don't get wet at two fishy attractions – an Oceanarium and Marine Life Centre – at St David's.

You can also visit woollen mills which produce colourful Welsh tapestries, museums of all kinds, and special-interest attractions such as the Pembrokeshire Motor Museum's display of old vehicles near Haverfordwest. There's even the chance to spend a morning watching Welsh cheese being made the traditional way at the Llangloffan Farmhouse Cheese Centre near Fishguard.

Mumbles Pier

Mumbles

Map Ref **D5**

Strangely named Mumbles is a busy little sailing and watersports centre on the western flank of Swansea Bay. The pier – a popular fishing spot – and seafront amenities help preserve its character, essentially that of a Victorian seaside resort. The rocks and lighthouse at Mumbles Head mark the start of the Gower Peninsula – just around the corner are the pleasant little bays of Bracelet and Limeslade.

Oystermouth Castle, in an elevated grassy setting above Mumbles and the bay, guards the landward approach to the peninsula. This stronghold, dating from the 13th century yet still standing to its original height, has worn very well.

Myddfai

Map Ref **E3**

This traditional village, in the untravelled hills south of Llandovery, was the home of the Physicians of Myddfai, celebrated throughout medieval Wales for their cures. When we delve deeper into the story we discover a curious conjunction of fact and folk tale. The 'Lady of the Lake' from nearby Llyn y Fan Fach (see entry) is said to have left sons with remarkable healing powers.

Narberth

Map Ref **B4**

The little town of Narberth has a surprisingly large entry in this guide. The space devoted to it reflects the concentration of tourist attractions which has grown up in the surrounding countryside – everything from farm parks to Wales's answer to the American theme park.

But first, let's look at Narberth itself. The town, with its attractive shops, Georgian features and ruined castle (in private ownership), remains true to its roots as a modest market centre and meeting place for country folk. In the Dark Ages, Narberth was one of the homes of the princes of Dyfed, and is mentioned in the *Mabinogion*, the early collection of Welsh folk tales. The town stands on the Landsker, a ghostly line (you'll not find it on any map) which separates the 'Little England beyond Wales' of south Pembrokeshire from the more traditional 'Welshry' to the north. Local history is the theme at the town's Wilson Museum, housed in an interesting old building which preserves part of a public bar.

Of the many places to visit nearby, Oakwood Park draws the biggest audience. The park, one of Wales's largest

Places to visit

Mumbles
Mumbles Pier
Tel (01792) 368197 C
Superb views across Swansea Bay. Amusements.

Oystermouth Castle
Tel (01792) 635444 C
Exceptionally well preserved, with decorative touches, including beautiful windows.

Places to visit

Narberth
Wilson Museum of Narberth
Tel (01834) 861266 C
Well-presented exhibits on local history and culture – old photographs, costumes, bygones.

Nearby
Black Pool Mill and Caverns,
Canaston Bridge (on minor road off A4075 3 miles west of Narberth)
Tel (01437) 541233 C
Wheels still turn. Attractive walks from mill.

Canaston Centre, Canaston Bridge
Tel (01834) 891622 C
Crystal Maze, tenpin bowling, adventure games room. Close to Oakwood Park.

Heron's Brook Animal and Bird Park
(on minor road off A478 about 1 mile south-west of Narberth)
Tel (01834) 860723 C
A 'down on the farm' experience. Pony rides, woodland walk, maze, cowboy town. Watch out for the goats when you're eating your picnic!

(continued overleaf)

Narberth

Nearby

Llawhaden Castle
(off A40 3 miles north-west of Narberth) F
Decorative and military features.

**Oakwood Park, Canaston Bridge
(off A4075 2½ miles south-west of Narberth)
Tel (01834) 891376/891373** C
Park your car and ride by miniature train into the adventure and leisure park. Over 40 attractions, including go-karts, novelty rides, gold rush town, boating lake and Megafobia rollercoaster.

Oakwood Park, near Narberth

tourist attractions, is organized along the latest lines. Visitors pay one admission charge on entry which covers unlimited use of the many rides and attractions within the 32-hectare (80-acre) park, including Europe's largest wooden roller coaster.

Things are a little more peaceful at the Heron's Brook Animal and Bird Park. Set in a delightful grassy valley, Heron's Brook is the home of a huge variety of ducks, geese, pheasants and bantams, not to mention the cattle, sheep, goats and pigs.

Black Pool Mill and Caverns stand in a tranquil spot on the upper reaches of the Eastern Cleddau. The four-storeyed building, put up in 1813, is one of Britain's finest remaining water-driven mills. Its caverns contain life-size copies of extinct wild animals and a huge Welsh dragon.

Nearby is Llawhaden Castle, a little-known historic site in a commanding position overlooking Pembrokeshire's green farmlands. Originally a basic military stronghold, it evolved over the years into a fortified palace for the bishops of St David's.

Llawhaden Castle

Neath

**Gnoll Country Park
Tel (01639) 635808** F
Large moss house gardens with grottos, streams and follies. Cascades down wooded slope. Ice house, visitor centre, reservoir, forest paths. Close to town centre - signposted off B4287 Cimla Road.

Neath Abbey F
Extensive ruins of monastery founded in 1130 and once called 'the fairest abbey in all Wales'. Industrial vandals of late 18th century used it as iron foundry; now clean and serene despite proximity to Neath Industrial Estate.

Neath Castle F
Part of gatehouse and flanking towers remain of 13th-century stronghold near town centre.

**Neath Museum, Orchard Street
Tel (01639) 645741** C
Varied exhibits include finds from local Roman fort, Nidum, and life-size model of Roman cavalryman.

Aberdulais Falls, near Neath

Neath

Map Ref **E5**

This pleasant town – gateway to the attractive Vale of Neath – has tended to be overshadowed by neighbouring Swansea. But it has a character all of its own, and those who seek it out are rewarded by some unexpected delights. There is, for example, its museum, housed in a beautiful building that was once the home of a man who worked with Darwin on the theory of evolution.

The town centre is pedestrianized and an indoor market adds variety to the scene. A notable event in the sporting world is commemorated by the plaque outside the Castle Hotel stating that the inaugural meeting of the Welsh Rugby Union was held there in March 1881. Neath continues to have strong links with Wales's national sport: Neath Rugby Club – the Welsh All Blacks – has played a notable part in the development of the game in Wales.

Neath is close to the Penscynor Wildlife Park, a major tourist attraction, and Aberdulais Falls, a National Trust site that combines industrial heritage with natural beauty. Opposite the falls is the Aberdulais Basin, a once-busy junction of the Neath and Tennant canals, where you can enjoy quiet towpath walks and see a unique skew bridge and 103m- (340ft) long aqueduct over the River Neath. Boat trips are available on a restored section of the Neath Canal. A large folk festival is held every August in nearby Pontardawe.

There is a Tourist Information Centre a mile or so west of Neath at Llandarcy (just off Junction 43 of the M4 motorway).

Penscynor Wildlife Park, near Neath

Newcastle Emlyn

Map Ref **C3**

Newcastle Emlyn is a flourishing little country and market town in the beautiful Teifi Valley with plenty of inns and a good range of shops. It stands at a meeting of routes on the boundary between the counties of Carmarthenshire and Cardiganshire and has an air of importance unrelated to its size.

The place is full of character, with fascinating byways and some interesting architecture: fine town houses where local dignitaries lived in style are now banks; a Victorian Town Hall in Market Place with a picturesque clock tower; and Bethel Chapel, built near the parish church in 1820, a good example of chapel architecture of that period.

One of the most attractive features of the town is the variety of river views it offers. Some of the best of these can be obtained from the castle ruins, a short walk from Market Place. Here one can clearly see how the town has been built above a broad loop in the River Teifi, bordering a valley to the south which is a serene patchwork of woods and meadows.

Newgale

Map Ref **A4**

Surfers and holidaymakers in search of wide, open sandy spaces head for Newgale in the far west of Pembrokeshire. The beach, on St Bride's Bay, is huge. Access is good – the main road runs alongside the beach, protected from the sea by a bank of shingle. Newgale itself is no more than a small village, completely dwarfed by its 2-mile beach.

Places to visit

Neath

Nearby
Aberdulais Falls 🌾
(just off A465 2 miles north-east of Neath)
Tel (01639) 636674 C
Lovely waterfalls in small wooded gorge ½ mile from Penscynor Wildlife Park. Remains of 19th-century tinplate works powered by falls. Largest electricity-generating waterwheel in Europe. Visitor centre interprets history of site. Car park opposite Dulais Rock Inn. Aberdulais Basin nearby (follow signs to basin, nr Railway Tavern).

Penscynor Wildlife Park
Tel (01639) 642189 C
Exotic birds and animals in beautiful wooded park on hillside 2 miles from Neath, off A465. Free-flying birds in tropical house, families of monkeys, sea lions, penguins, flamingos. Aquaria, chairlift to alpine slide, adventure playground. A very popular family attraction.

Places to visit

Newcastle Emlyn

Newcastle Emlyn Castle F
Scanty ruins of the 'new' castle of 1240, parts of the gatehouse and a few walls remaining on a grassy knoll.

Nearby
Museum of the Welsh NMGW
Woollen Industry, Dre-fach Felindre (off A484 3 miles south-east of Newcastle Emlyn)
Tel (01559) 370929 C
Recalls the great days of woollen manufacture in the Teifi Valley. Interpretive centre with craft workshops and operational woollen mill on site. Extensive collection of tools and equipment, including spinning mules and carding engines.

Teifi Valley Railway, Henllan (3 miles east of Newcastle Emlyn on A484)
Tel (01559) 371077 C
Steam and diesel trains run 1½ miles along narrow-gauge line through woodland. Tiny engine shed open to public. Playgrounds, nature trail, amphitheatre.

Newport

Your tour of Newport should really start at the top of Stow Hill, just over ¼ mile from the shopping centre. The town, Wales's third largest conurbation, is built on a succession of hills around the tidal mouth of the River Usk. The past importance of Newport's docks, which accounted for the town's 19th-century growth as a coal- and iron-exporting port, is plain to see from Stow Hill's lofty vantage point. Spread out to the south is a vast area of wharves and warehouses, dominated by a structure that has become synonymous with the Newport skyline. This is the town's famous Transporter Bridge built early this century across the Usk. An ingenious device, it carries vehicles across the river on an aerial gondola suspended from its main span.

Stow Hill is crowned by an ancient religious site. St Woolos Cathedral stands on ground which has witnessed religious worship since the 6th century. You enter through an endearing little chapel, clearly at odds with its more grandiose big brother, the main cathedral building. The chapel, which shows signs of Anglo-Saxon stonework, is linked to the rest of the cathedral by a fine Norman archway.

Newport's original castle also stood on this site. A new stone castle was built down the hill by the side of the river in the 14th century. Its ruined shell now looks forlorn and out of place amongst the roads and modern developments on the approach to the town centre.

The town's modern heart is centred around John Frost Square, an area named after a leader of Newport's 1839 Chartist Uprising which called for electoral reform and ended in bloody confrontation when troops killed over 20 Chartists. A huge mosaic mural leading from the square depicts the march and its bloody outcome.

The story of the march is recalled in Newport's Museum and Art Gallery, located in the square. This imaginatively laid-out museum covers a number of themes – archaeology, industrial history, wildlife and so on. Its 'four seasons' Roman mosaic floor from nearby Caerwent is particularly impressive.

The murals in the Civic Centre are another visual treat. The entrance hall houses 11 striking murals of heroic proportions depicting scenes from early Celtic times to the 1960s. Back in the centre of town, don't miss the covered market, a delightful piece of Victoriana. Completed in 1899 and surmounted by a lofty tower and spire, this iron-and-glass structure has a barrel-vaulted roof and stalls on

The Transporter Bridge, Newport

Tredegar House, on the outskirts of Newport

Places to visit

Newport

Fourteen Locks Canal Centre
Rogerstone (on western outskirts near junction 27 of M4)
Tel (01633) 894802 F
Canal exhibition, picnic site, waymarked walks.

Newport Castle F
Remains include central tower, watergate and decorative windows. For the best view, walk across the bridge and look back at the castle's river frontage.

Newport Centre, Kingsway
Tel (01633) 841522 C
Excellent leisure and entertainment centre. Pool, sports, concerts.

Newport Museum and Art Gallery, John Frost Square
Tel (01633) 84006 F
Largest provincial museum in Wales.

St Woolos Cathedral
Evidence of Norman – and even earlier – architectural influences. Robust castellated tower of c.1500.

Tredegar House (on western edge of town near junction 28 of M4)
Tel (01633) 815880. House and Gardens C Grounds F
Guided tours of 'architectural wonder of Wales'. Crafts, boating lake, carriage rides, restored orangery.

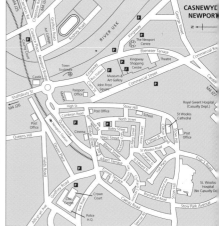

ground-floor and balcony levels selling everything from fresh vegetables to second-hand comics. On the High Street nearby is the tall, half-timbered Murenger House, now a pub. Dating from 1530, it is one of the few survivors from old, pre-industrial Newport.

We have to travel to the outskirts of town to discover a pre-eminent historic site that captures the flavour of a vanished age. Red-bricked Tredegar House, standing in 36-hectare (90-acre) grounds, is a magnificent 17th-century mansion which was the home of the powerful Morgan family. Family and house rode on the crest of a wave thanks to the fortunes created by Newport's booming 19th-century docklands. But in addition to the glittering splendour of its 'upstairs', Tredegar House also preserves its 'below stairs' where an army of servants worked.

Also on the outskirts to the west of Newport is the Fourteen Locks Canal Centre. The centre stands at the top of a monumental Victorian engineering feat – a huge staircase of locks that allowed barges to be raised and lowered up and down a steep hillside.

Newport (Pembrokeshire) Map Ref B3

This ancient town stands a stone's throw from Newport Bay. The seashore here has something for everyone – along Newport Beach and Parrog (Newport's old 'port') you'll find a mixture of long, firm sands, rock pools, dunes and pebbles. Newport's small size belies its historic role. It received its town charter in the 13th century, was an administrative centre for a local barony and still has a mayor, who is involved with various long-standing ceremonies including the annual 'beating of the bounds'. Newport Castle is of Norman origin. Its ruined gatehouse was restored as a private residence in 1859.

Newport's surrounding hills and rocky seashores are dense with historic – and prehistoric – sites (far too many to mention all of them here). The most famous is the Pentre Ifan Cromlech, a burial chamber built around 3–4000BC in the foothills of the Preselis. A stark collection of angular upright stones supports a massive 5m (16ft) capstone across the roof of the chamber. Originally, the monument would have been covered by an earthen mound. Pentre Ifan is made of the same Preseli 'bluestones' which also found their way – somehow – to Stonehenge on Salisbury Plain nearly 200 miles away.

The rocky ridge above Newport is occupied by Carningli Iron Age hillfort, while one of King Arthur's 1001 claimed burial places is said to be beneath the giant sloping capstone of Carreg Coetan Arthur in the town itself. The churchyard at Nevern, a pretty village nearby, contains a 'bleeding' yew tree and 1000-year-old Celtic cross decorated with intricate interlacing designs.

Visiting ancient sites takes on a whole new meaning at Castell Henllys Iron Age Fort. Castell Henllys recreates living conditions as they would have been over 2000 years ago. The centrepiece of the site is a tall roundhouse made of oak and reeds, with smaller structures – such as a forge and goat house – ranged around it.

Places to visit

Newport
Carreg Coetan Arthur
Burial Chamber F
Prehistoric site with sloping capstone.

Newport Castle
In private ownership. View from outside only.

Nearby
Castell Henllys Iron Age Fort (off A487 about 4 miles east of Newport)
Tel (01239) 891319 C
Iron Age life recreated.

Nevern Churchyard Cross F
One of Wales's finest Celtic Crosses. Amazing carvings.

Pentre Ifan Cromlech
(3 miles south-east of Newport on minor road signposted off A487) F
One of Wales's finest prehistoric burial chambers.

The north Pembrokeshire coast at Newport

Neyland

Neyland is an old seafaring town and railway port of neat terraces on a hillside above the Milford Haven waterway. Its links with the sea have been given a fresh injection of life thanks to the building of a 300-berth marina on a long, narrow inlet, lined by wooded banks, just off the main waterway.

The waterfront is called Brunel Quay in memory of that great Victorian engineer, Isambard Kingdom Brunel, whose Great Western Railway reached Neyland in 1856 (a remaining section of railway line can be seen along the edge of the quay). From here, passengers sailed on to Southern Ireland. The Cleddau Bridge, a crucial road link between the south and north banks of the waterway, looms over the quayside. Opened in 1975, it replaced the ferry that used to run between Neyland and Hobb's Point. Nearby Hazelbeach (at Llanstadwell) is a small, rocky beach below low cliffs.

The marina at Neyland

Places to visit

Ogmore-by-Sea

Ogmore Castle F

Shell of an important Norman stronghold in picturesque setting.

Ogmore-by-Sea

The village is perched on headlands above the mouth of the River Ogmore. Ogmore Castle guards the confluence of the Ogmore and Ewenny rivers. To the Norman warlords, this was a strategically important fording point – you can still cross the shallow Ewenny on a series of stepping stones. The castle is an early one, dating from the 11th century. Originally built of earth and timber (later to be replaced by stone), it served as the power base for William de Londres ('of London').

Ogmore stands on Glamorgan's Heritage Coast, a 14-mile stretch of ruggedly beautiful cliff-backed seashore which runs between Porthcawl and Aberthaw east of Llantwit Major.

Places to visit

Oxwich

Oxwich Castle

Tel (01792) 390359 C

Comfortable family mansion dating from Tudor times, with impressive Elizabethan additions.

Oxwich

Oxwich is one of the Gower Peninsula's popular south-coast beaches. The bay is fringed by a glorious 3-mile stretch of sands backed by a high barrier of dunes. A large car park is located right next to the beach – which helps to explain Oxwich's popularity. But the beauty of the surroundings is the main magnet. In addition to beach and dunes, there are woods along the headland leading to Oxwich Point, and a reedy stretch of salt- and freshwater marsh.

Most of this varied habitat is within the Oxwich National Nature Reserve. There is an information centre in the car park, and visitors can follow paths through the reserve. One walk into the oak and ash woods along the headland passes St Illtud's Church, of 13th century origin. Oxwich's 'castle', on the hill above with views across the bay, is in reality a grand Tudor house with mock-military embellishments.

Oxwich Bay

Three Cliffs Bay, accessible from Parkmill

Parkmill

Map Ref **D5**

Historic sites from different eras in Gower's history stand in or close to Parkmill. Gower's rural heritage is recalled at a restored corn mill in the village. Amongst the sandy burrows to the south, overlooking lovely Three Cliffs Bay, are the long-abandoned ruins of Pennard Castle. Sand blows through the courtyard of a castle whose most upstanding features are its stumpy gate towers.

A lane north-west from the village leads to a grassy, hidden valley that has been inhabited by man since prehistoric times. Neolithic (New Stone Age) inhabitants built Parc le Breos, a stone burial chamber around 6000 years old whose foundations can still be seen. A little further up the valley is an even older site. Cathole Cave, which contained bones of mammoth and woolly rhinoceros, was inhabited towards the end of the Ice Age about 10,000 years ago.

Places to visit

Parkmill

Parc le Breos Burial Chamber F
1/2 mile from village.

Pennard Castle F
Fragmentary ruins on edge of golf links.

Y Felin Ddŵr
Tel (01792) 371206 C
Craft, countryside and Gower heritage centre based at an old farm and restored watermill.

Partrishow's rood screen

Church and churchyard are fascinating

Partrishow

Map Ref **G4**

You'll have to scan the map to find Partrishow; and you'll have to search the lanes in the hills above Abergavenny to find tiny Partrishow Church. The effort is well worth it, for this gem of a church contains an exceptional rood screen, possibly the finest in Wales. The delicate, highly elaborate screen, carved in Irish oak, was the work of fastidious, highly skilled Tudor craftsmen. The isolated church evokes a strong sense of the past. Dating from the 11th century, it also contains a Norman font and macabre wall painting of a skeleton depicting death.

A cul-de-sac road to the north leads though the forested slopes of the remote Grwyne Fawr Valley, where you'll find attractive picnic sites and walks to a remote mountain reservoir.

Places to visit

Partrishow

Partrishow Church
Isolated, atmospheric religious site, rich in history.

Walking

There are walks to suit all tastes in South Wales. Enthusiasts can set off on strenuous long-distance hikes. There are short waymarked trails and gentle woodland paths for fair-weather walkers and families. South Wales's most famous walk, the Pembrokeshire Coast Path, suits everyone. If you want a challenge, see if you can beat the 3½ days which is the claimed record for walking its entire 186 miles. Most visitors, though, are content to follow short stretches of this magnificent coastal footpath.

The Brecon Beacons National Park is incomparable walking country. The appeal of the Beacons lies in the rare sense of freedom and space walkers find amongst huge areas of open hillsides. As with Pembrokeshire, there's something here for all levels of walker. The Beacons' extensive stretches of wild upland should be treated with the utmost respect – this terrain is for experienced, well-equipped walkers. For casual walkers, there are gentler trails (from the Brecon Beacons Mountain Centre near Libanus, for example – a good source, of walking information) and woodland paths in the forests along the southern flanks of the park.

The Offa's Dyke Path, another long distance walk, runs from South to North Wales for 168 miles. The Wye Valley along the Wales/England border is particularly attractive to walkers: not only does the Offa's Dyke Path run along the ridge above the valley, but there are also many other paths to follow,

including the lowland Wye Valley Walk and local trails through the woods.

There are many attractive walks through the richly varied landscape of the border country. The Usk Valley Walk, for example, runs for 25 miles between Caerleon and Abergavenny, while the 26-mile Newport to Tredegar Sirhowy Valley Walk crosses the undulating valleys of South Wales. Long-distance walks in other parts of the South Wales Valleys include the Coed Morgannwg Way, Ogwr Ridgeway Walk and Taff-Ely Ridgeway Walk.

There are coastal walks along the Gower Peninsula, towpath walks beside the Monmouthshire and Brecon Canal, a programme of guided walks in the Brecon Beacons and Pembrokeshire, walks in the woods, walks in the country ... far too many to include here. Ask for details at Tourist Information Centres.

Pembrey/Burry Port

Map Ref **D4**

Pembrey and Burry Port are neighbouring towns on the A484 west of Swansea, overlooking the Burry Inlet and the open waters of Carmarthen Bay. The area is no stranger to visitors – local attractions include a huge beach, popular country park and thriving motor sports racetrack.

Burry Port, which grew up in the days of coal and tinplate manufacture, has a large and unexpectedly pretty harbour filled with holiday craft. Walk along the quayside wall to the harbour mouth for a magnificent view across the Burry Inlet to the shores of the Gower Peninsula opposite. The waterfront is part of the far-reaching Millennium Coastal Park scheme, a project due for completion in 2000 (see Llanelli entry for details).

The dunes bordering the harbour mark the start of the vast 7-mile-long Cefn Sidan Sands. This is one beach that never gets crowded, despite the popularity of the Pembrey Country Park, an unconventional park that includes part of Cefn Sidan together with large areas of conifer forest and grassland.

The park offers easy access to the beach (there's plenty of car parking next to the sands). Other attractions here include forest walks, a dry ski slope, birdwatching, children's play areas, picnic sites, pony trekking and a narrow-gauge railway. Nearby is the Welsh Motor Sports Centre, a popular weekend venue for a wide variety of four- and two-wheel competitive events, and a regular testing track with top Formula One teams.

Pembrey's churchyard contains a monument to a French soldier and his daughter Adeline, 'niece of Josephine, Consort to the renowned individual Napoleon Bonaparte'. Father and daughter were drowned in a shipwreck off Cefn Sidan Sands. Look out too for the old animal pound – a rare survivor – by the churchyard gate.

Pembroke/ Pembroke Dock

Map Ref **B5**

Pembroke's mighty castle is not the only reminder of this town's historic pedigree. Surviving stretches of 14th-century walls – remarkably well preserved in parts – enclose the narrow ridge on which the main body of the town stands. Pembroke Castle was an early power base for the Norman invaders. Its present appearance is due to William Marshall, an influential English knight who rebuilt the fortress in the late 12th and early 13th centuries.

His magnificent castle, on a wooded outcrop above the streets and river, remains unaltered to this day. Its size only becomes fully apparent when you walk through its Great Gatehouse. The castle walls enclose a large, grassy inner ward dominated by the Great Keep, a huge round tower nearly 24m (80ft) high. Climb to the top for the definitive view of the town. One of the smaller towers protecting the main walls was the reputed birthplace of Harri Tudur, the Welshman who became Henry VII, first of the Tudors. The

Places to visit

Pembrey/Burry Port

Pembrey Country Park
Tel (01554) 833913 C
210-hectare (520-acre) park. Great variety of activities – everything from swimming to dry slope skiing and toboggan ride. Visitor centre contains exhibition on park.

The Pembrey Country Park boasts a huge beach and wide range of attractions

Places to visit

Pembroke/Pembroke Dock

Museum of the Home, 7 Westgate Hill
Tel (01646) 681200 C
An amazing collection of everyday items. Thousands of things to see.

Pembroke Castle
Tel (01646) 681510 C
One of Wales's finest medieval castles. Impressive Great Keep.

Nearby
Lamphey Bishop's Palace C
Large house – a most sumptuous residence in its time – which was a country retreat for the bishops of St David's.

Upton Castle Grounds (on minor road off A477 3 miles north-east of Pembroke) F
Tranquil, beautiful gardens in sheltered valley. Over 250 different species of trees and shrubs, flower beds, terraces, small chapel. Castle not open to the public.

Pembroke Castle's Great Keep

hill opposite the castle, now occupied by cavernous Monkton Church, was the site of a medieval priory.

The Museum of the Home, on the street below the castle walls, is packed full of everyday items from the ordinary home spanning the last 300 years. This remarkable collection of over 3000 exhibits covers games and toys, cleaning, cooking, sewing, lighting, reading, smoking and snuff taking ... and more besides! The town's long and turbulent history is featured in interpretive displays at the 'Gateway to Pembroke' visitor centre (part of the Tourist Information Centre).

Pembroke Dock stands on the Milford Haven waterway a mile or so north-west of Pembroke. The town, whose streets conform to a rigid 'grid-iron' plan, was an important 19th-century shipbuilding and naval base. Today, Pembroke Dock is an Irish Sea ferry port.

The port stands at a dividing line in the great Milford Haven waterway. Downstream, the banks are occupied by the historic naval docklands, Napoleonic fortifications and giant oil and petro-chemical installations fed by massive supertankers. Upriver, there is a completely different world, the unspoilt creeks and wooded shores of the Daugleddau. Pembroke Dock's fascinating maritime and military history is told at the Tourist Information Centre, housed in a restored 19th-century guntower.

Places to visit

Penarth

Penarth Pier
Tel (01222) 708212 F
Victorian pier restored to its former glory.

Turner House Art Gallery, NMGW
Plymouth Road
Tel (01222) 708870 C
Regular exhibitions from National Museums and Galleries of Wales collections but some blank weeks. Check before going.

Nearby

Cosmeston Lakes Country Park
(off B4267 between Penarth and Barry)
Tel (01222) 701678 F
More than 80 hectares (200 acres) of lakes, woodlands and meadows. Rich plant and bird life. Adventure playground, bridleways, picnic sites.

Cosmeston Medieval Village
Tel (01222) 701678 C
14th-century village reconstructed on its original foundations. Cottages, barn, farmyard animals, costumed guides, special events. In grounds of country park.

Penarth Pier

Penarth

Map Ref **G6**

There is still something genteel and other-worldly about this small seaside resort, which keeps daintily aloof from big-brother Cardiff, a mere 4 miles away. The Victorian pier is an intrinsic part of Penarth's charm. Cafés and restaurants to suit all pockets line the promenade, and there are colourful parks and a pleasant cliff walk, with views of Flat Holm and Steep Holm islands. The old coal-exporting dock has been transformed into the Penarth Portway Marina, with 400 berths. Paddle-steamer trips run from the pier in summer.

Penclawdd

Map Ref **D5**

The fresh cockles on sale at Swansea Market come from the sands off Penclawdd on Gower's northern shores. Penclawdd's tidal sandbanks are Wales's most famous cockle beds – and the hardy Penclawdd cockle gatherers, who hand-pick cockles as they follow the falling tide with their buckets and carts, are something of a national institution.

The Gower Peninsula's low-lying northern coastline is completely different to the limestone cliffs and sandy bays of the south. The contrast is at its most emphatic along Llanrhidian Marsh, an eerie expanse of saltings and marshland a few miles west of Penclawdd. The marsh is overlooked by Weobley Castle, whose well-preserved late 13th-century walls enclose a small courtyard.

Places to visit

Penclawdd
Nearby
Weobley Castle, nr Llanrhidian
Tel (01792) 390012 C
More a fortified manor house than castle.
Exhibition. Superb viewpoint.

Cockle pickers at Penclawdd

Pendine

Map Ref **C4**

A flat, wide sandy beach stretches eastwards from Pendine as far as the eye can see. Pendine's vast 6-mile beach was the scene of land speed record attempts in the daredevil early days of motoring. In the 1920s, Sir Malcolm Campbell in *Blue Bird* and the Welsh ace J G Parry Thomas in *Babs* battled to become the world's fastest man on four wheels. In 1927, the unfortunate Parry Thomas met his death here while trying to better his rival's 174.88mph.

The wrecked *Babs,* which was buried in the sand dunes, was dug up in 1971 and restored to full working order by a motoring enthusiast. The 'Sands of Speed' story is told at Pendine's Museum of Speed. Amongst the other record-breakers attracted to Pendine was aviator Amy Johnson, who took off from here in 1933 on her flight across the Atlantic. The Ministry of Defence now controls part of the sands, so access is limited – but don't worry, there's still plenty of this giant-sized beach left for you and me!

Places to visit

Pendine
Museum of Speed
Tel (01994) 453488 C
Display of record-breaking and other fast vehicles.

Pont Nedd Fechan

Map Ref **F4**

This little village, tucked away at the head of the Neath Valley near Glyn Neath, is a marvellous walking centre. The walks from the village are not of the usual hill and mountain variety. Pont Nedd Fechan has some of the most intriguing walks in Wales. Start off by the bridge in the middle of the village and follow the banks of the rivers Neath and Pyrddin for a mile or so through a wooded gorge to Sgwd Gwladys, one of the many spectacular waterfalls in this area (see Ystradfellte entry for more details).

Other walks start at Craig y Ddinas (Dinas Rock), a giant outcrop ½ mile east of the village. From here, you can follow the courses of the rivers Mellte and Sychryd to abandoned gunpowder works and silica mines, set in rugged countryside of great natural beauty.

Pontsticill

Map Ref **F4**

This village, a few miles north of Merthyr Tydfil, is surrounded by upland scenery on a grand scale. A string of lovely reservoirs extends northwards into the heart of the Brecon Beacons. The nearest – Taf-fechan – is a popular sailing venue and lakeside halt on the narrow-gauge Brecon Mountain Railway (see Merthyr Tydfil entry).

Taf-fechan reservoir, Pontsticill

Blaen-y-glyn waterfall in the mountains above Pontsticill

A minor road north leads to the remote Neuadd reservoir, set in a bowl beneath the Beacons' highest peaks. An old stony trackway, which may have been a Roman road, runs northwards along the shoulder of the reservoir to the 'Gap', a 598m (1962ft) break in the spine of the mountains before descending towards Brecon.

There's a good choice of forest walks from car parks beside the scenic road which climbs over the mountains to Talybont on Usk. From the car park near the summit, a trail leads to the Blaen-y-glyn waterfall.

Pontypool   Map Ref **G4**

Like many another town in South Wales, Pontypool has made a new life for itself after the passing of the industries that once flourished there. For over 200 years, the Hanbury family played a dominant role in its fortunes. Early in the 18th century, John Hanbury made Pontypool the first centre of commercial tinplate production in Britain. Its reputation was such that the first American ironworks drew on equipment and skilled workers from the town.

Pontypool has some interesting buildings, including the Town Hall built by Capel Hanbury Leigh to commemorate the birth of his son and heir in 1853 (when he was aged 77!). The handsomely gabled Market House in pedestrianized Commercial Street dates from 1730 and the indoor market nearby still displays an old notice setting out the tolls paid in bygone days.

The pleasantly wooded Pontypool Park runs downhill opposite the Town Hall. Walk through it to reach the Valley Inheritance Museum, an industrial heritage interpretive centre splendidly housed in the former stable block of the Hanbury mansion. The parks leisure facilities include an indoor swimming pool and excellent dry ski slope with long main run.

Pontymoile Canal Basin, with its aqueduct and tollkeeper's cottage, is east of the road out of town towards Newport. One of the more pleasant spots within easy reach is Llandegfedd reservoir, set in the low wooded hills between Pontypool and Usk. A host of activities takes place on and around this scenic stretch of water, including windsurfing, sailing, canoeing and fly fishing. There is also a picnic area for viewing wildfowl.

Sailing is popular at Llandegfedd reservoir near Pontypool

Pontypridd

Map Ref **F5**

This busy valleys town recalls its past at the Pontypridd
Historical and Cultural Centre. The centre, in an
imaginatively converted chapel next to a famous 18th-
century single-arched stone bridge, tells the story of
Pontypridd's heyday during the coal era. The town is still
very much alive – especially if you come when the streets
are packed with shoppers and stallholders during
Wednesday and Saturday market days.

Pontypridd provides plenty of evidence to support
Wales's 'land of song' image. It is Tom Jones's home town,
and nearby Cilfynydd was the birthplace of singers Stewart
Burrows and the late Sir Geraint Evans. In Ynysangharad
Park near the town centre there are two statues
commemorating father and son Evan and James James,
writers of the Welsh National Anthem. Wales's addiction to
rugby was the inspiration behind the John Hughes Grogg
Shop. John Hughes's unique sculptures of famous rugby
players led to worldwide fame for his 'groggs', which now
depict everyone from sporting personalities to pop stars
and politicians.

Places to visit

Pontypridd

John Hughes Grogg Shop, Broadway
Tel (01443) 405001 F
Rugby players, showbiz stars,
politicians, all receiving the 'grogg'
treatment.

**Pontypridd Historical and Cultural
Centre, Bridge Street**
Tel (01443) 409512 C
Wide-ranging local museum housed in
old chapel.

Port Eynon

Map Ref **D5**

The Gower Peninsula's succession of south-facing sandy
bays ends at the old smugglers haunt of Port Eynon. A
curtain of cliffs unfolds beyond the beach, stretching all the
way to Rhossili at the western tip of the peninsula. Port
Eynon's pretty crescent of sands is a popular spot in
summer (the bay is also accessible from the neighbouring
village of Horton).

Culver Hole, on the headland, is a mysterious walled-up
fissure in the cliffs which no one seems to be able to
explain. The headland also contains the ruins of the Salt
House, a mansion reputedly destroyed in a great storm 300
years ago. A spectacular cliff walk leads westwards above a
remote shoreline for about 5 miles to Rhossili and Worms
Head, Gower's exposed western tip. On the way, the path
passes Paviland Cave (access is dangerous) where
prehistoric bones were found together with flint tools and
the remains of elephant and mammoth.

Port Eynon

Porthcawl

Map Ref **E5**

This popular seaside resort has something for everyone.
Families who want all the fun of the fair and sandy
'bucket-and-spade' beaches head for Sandy Bay and Trecco
Bay. Those looking for quieter times will find them around
the headland along the attractively remodelled Esplanade,
grassy Lock's Common and aptly named Rest Bay.

Porthcawl is a resort with a dual personality. The bright
lights and best beaches are along its eastern shores. Firm,
flat and spacious sands front the shoreline, next to the rides
and amusements of the Coney Beach Pleasure Park and
extensive caravan holiday home parks. Porthcawl's
picturesque harbour – a popular spot with fishermen – is
the dividing line between the popular and the more
peaceful. From here, the Esplanade curves around a rocky
foreshore to the sands and rock pools of Rest Bay.

Further north-west again is the Kenfig Pool and Dunes
National Nature Reserve, based around the dunes of the
Kenfig Burrows. The freshwater 28-hectare (70-acre) pool,

Places to visit

Porthcawl

Coney Beach Pleasure Park
Tel (01656) 788911
Large funfair. Great choice of rides and
amusements.

Porthcawl Museum, John Street
Tel (01656) 782211 C
Homely little museum with displays on
geology, costumes and memorabilia of
old Porthcawl.

The Esplanade, Porthcawl

and the sand dunes which enclose it, are an important habitat for wildlife. The reserve, which contains a visitor centre, stands over a buried medieval borough which became gradually overwhelmed by sand.

Amongst the shops off Porthcawl's Esplanade is a small local museum (next to the Tourist Information Centre). The refurbished Grand Pavilion, on the front, stages a wide variety of entertainments throughout the year. Porthcawl's shores are popular with watersports enthusiasts and fishermen, though the resort's most famous sporting feature is the challenging Royal Porthcawl Golf Club, where top competitions are held.

At Newton on the eastern fringes of Porthcawl a large, pleasant green, bordered by a church, gives the area the look of an English village. The shores bordering Newton are at the western end of the Glamorgan Heritage Coast, a 14-mile stretch of unspoilt dunelands and cliffs. Nottage on the northern approach to Porthcawl is rich in historic interest.

Porth-gain
Map Ref **A3**

If Pembrokeshire conjures up only images of coastal beauty untouched by the hand of man, then go to Porth-gain on its rocky northern shores. Many visitors find Porth-gain beautiful, but in an unconventional, strange way. Its perfectly sheltered little harbour is dominated by the shell of a building in which stones were crushed. The hoppers along the quayside are more reminders of Porth-gain's unexpected industrial past. Stone, quarried on the cliffs nearby, was brought to this harbour for shipment to Britain's growing industrial cities in the booming 19th century. Old photographs in the Sloop Inn depict the quayside in its heyday.

The coast path across the headlands to the west skirts the abandoned quarries before arriving at Aber Eiddi, another intriguing spot. The quarries here – now flooded to form a shuddering deep 'Blue Lagoon' – produced slate. Remnants of workers' cottages can be seen above an unusual dark-sanded beach.

Pumsaint
Map Ref **E3**

The Romans were the first to arrive in this obscure spot deep in the hills. The lure was gold. Sleepy Pumsaint – no more than an inn, Post Office, handful of shops and houses – was the only place in Britain where the Romans are definitely known to have mined gold.

Serious mining began at Pumsaint's Dolaucothi Gold Mine in about AD75. A sophisticated system of mining, involving open-cast and underground workings together with miles of complex aqueducts, was soon producing Welsh gold for the imperial mint at Lyon. Clearly, Dolaucothi must have been important to the Romans, for they also built a fort – on ground now occupied by the Dolaucothi Arms Hotel – to protect their investment.

After the Romans' departure, Dolaucothi lay dormant for centuries. Revival in the 19th century did not last very long, the mines finally closing in 1938. Dolaucothi's fascinating story is told on the 'Miners' Way' self-guide surface trail and also on exciting guided underground tours.

A stone standing near the entrance to the mines explains Pumsaint's name. In English, pump saint means 'five

Exploring the Roman Gold Mines at Pumsaint

Places to visit

Pumsaint
Dolaucothi Roman Gold Mines
Tel (01558) 630359 C
Walks, guided tours, gold panning, visitor centre, display and video.

saints'. The five indentations on the stone are said to have been caused by five saints who used it as a communal pillow during a fierce storm which pressed their heads into the surface. As Welsh legends go, this tale is even taller than usual!

A National Trust visitor centre in the village serves as an introduction to the farm and woodland walks in the Trust's extensive Dolaucothi Estate, centred on the unspoilt Cothi Valley.

Raglan

Map Ref **H4**

Raglan Castle and the fortress at Chepstow 12 miles away stand at the opposite ends of the castle-building spectrum. Chepstow was Wales's – and Britain's – first stone-built castle, Raglan was one of the last. Their contrasting architecture reflects the changing times in Wales. Raglan is a product of the more settled 15th century, by which time military considerations could be diluted by a desire for creature comforts.

Raglan is more a palace than a castle. Its handsome towers, decorative flourishes, courts and state apartments can be seen as an expression of the social aspirations of its owners – look out, for example, for the huge fireplace and ornate windows in the hall, the finest of the castle's apartments. But it would be a mistake to regard Raglan as an effete pushover. The castle was subjected to one of the longest sieges of the Civil War, and its most outstanding feature – the damaged Great Tower – still stands despite attempts by Cromwell's engineers to demolish it.

Places to visit

Raglan
Raglan Castle
Tel (01291) 690228 C
Built in more peaceful later medieval period when emphasis could be given to decoration as well as defence.

Raglan Castle

Rhandirmwyn

Map Ref **E3**

Until the opening of the massive Llyn Brianne reservoir in the 1970s, Rhandirmwyn was an unknown village on the road to nowhere in the foothills of the Cambrian Mountains. The tarmac road, which petered out into a track in the wildernesses north of the village, now continues in spectacular fashion along the banks of the reservoir to link up with the Abergwesyn Pass.

So Rhandirmwyn is now on the map; but despite the increase in visitors, the village and its idyllic surroundings retain their air of away-from-it-all peace and tranquillity. It was not always so. The name Rhandirmwyn means 'lead mining area'. Surprisingly, this lovely valley was once the home of one of Europe's largest lead mines. Twm Siôn Cati, the 16th-century Welsh Robin Hood, hid amongst the rocks on Dinas Hill 2 miles north of the village. He evaded capture from the Sheriff of Carmarthen by hiding in a cave that can still be visited. Dinas Hill is now a Royal Society for the Protection of Birds reserve which can be explored by following a circular path from a small visitor centre beside the road on the eastern side of the hill. See if you can find Twm's cave, a detour off the path, hidden amongst the huge outcrops near the top of the hill.

Rhandirmwyn is in red kite country

Looking down into the Rhondda from the Bwlch y Clawdd mountain road

Rhondda

The Rhondda valleys – the Rhondda Fach (little) and Rhondda Fawr (big) – were synonymous with coalmining in the boom years of the 19th century. These narrow, steep-sided valleys were known far and wide as the source of the 'black diamond'. Tightly packed terraced communities, such as Treorchy and Treherbert, grew up alongside scores of mines in the confined valley floor – the only place where it was feasible to build.

How times have changed. The last pit in the Rhondda closed at the end of 1990. Massive land reclamation schemes have wiped away the debris of decades of intensive coalmining. The hillsides have been planted with conifer forests. The mountaintops, untouched by industry, remain wild, unspoilt places. To get a flavour of this unique part of Wales it's best to approach the Rhondda from one of the mountain roads which drop suddenly into the valleys – the spectacular A4061 Rhigos road from Hirwaun, for example, or the A4233 from Aberdare.

The mines have closed, but Rhondda's mining heritage has not disappeared. The Rhondda Heritage Park is based around the former Lewis Merthyr and Tŷ Mawr colliery sites at Trehafod, between Pontypridd and Porth. The extensive park contains mining equipment, colliery head-gear, a reconstructed village street and exhibition gallery. The 'Black Gold' story of the valleys' coalmining communities is brought to life through innovative multi-media displays, while the hardship and humour of working life underground are recreated in the 'Shift in Time' experience.

The abiding, surprising characteristic of these valleys is the way in which rural and industrial landscapes remain close neighbours. For a supreme example of this unexpected proximity, take the minor mountain road south-east from Ferndale. Within a matter of minutes, you are within the glades of the St Gwynno Forest which surround Llanwonno, a delightful hamlet based around an old church.

Worms Head, Rhossili

Rhossili

Rhossili is the 'Land's End' of Gower – and the land ends in a breathtakingly spectacular way. The village is perched on the edge of a severe cliff above a huge west-facing beach popular with surfers (the 3-mile beach can also be approached from Llangennith further north). Dylan Thomas often visited Rhossili, describing it as 'miles of yellow coldness going away into the distance of the sea'. The blackened stumps poking out from the sands are the remains of the *Helvetia*, a ship which ran aground here in 1887.

The furthest point west you can go is Worms Head, a narrow neck of land attached to mainland Gower by a low-tide causeway – so check the tide times before you walk across! A National Trust visitor centre at the start of the path contains displays on the area. There is a memorial in the village church to Petty Officer Edgar Evans, a native son of Rhossili who died in Scott's doomed Antarctic expedition of 1912.

St David's

When you first arrive at St David's, Britain's tiniest, most tranquil city, you'll be puzzled. The cathedral which gave St David's its city status is nowhere to be seen. This ancient cathedral settlement, the oldest in Britain, nestles discreetly in a grassy hollow beneath the rooftops. It stands on a monastic site founded by St David, Wales's patron saint, in the 6th century.

Those who know St David's may be surprised to discover that it was a 'veritable Piccadilly Circus' in the 5th and 6th centuries, a busy crossroads for those travelling by sea to Ireland, Cornwall and Brittany. In this Age of Saints, when devout missionaries spread the Christian message, no one was more dedicated than David. He chose a sheltered site for his community hidden away from any approach by land or sea yet conveniently close to the coast.

The size and stature of the present purple-stoned cathedral belies its humble origins. As it now stands, it dates from 1176. Although restored and improved over the ages, the cathedral remains, in essence, a magnificent example of medieval religious architecture and craftsmanship. Amongst its great glories are an ornately carved roof of Irish oak and the original late-Norman nave. This sacred site has been a place of pilgrimage for almost a thousand years, ever since a medieval pope decreed that two pilgrimages to St David's would equal one to Rome, with three accounting for one visit to Jerusalem.

The ruined Bishop's Palace in the field opposite now has the look of the poor relation, though in its prime it would have been a very grand and desirable residence indeed. Built in the 13th and 14th centuries, its opulent style reflected the worldly wealth of the medieval church.

You are never far from the sea at St David's. In the streets itself there are two 'fishy' attractions – the Marine Life Centre and an Oceanarium. Whitesand Bay, a mile or so to the north-west, is a superb sandy beach framed by rocky headlands. Exciting boat trips around Pembrokeshire's islands depart from here and Porthstinian (see below). The peninsula west of St David's is a magical place. A coast path winds its way around an indented shoreline of rock-bound coves, exposed cliffs and sheltered inlets teeming with birdlife.

The St Justinian Lifeboat Station squeezes itself in amongst the rocks at Porthstinian, a small harbour accessible by minor road west from St David's. Justinian was a 6th-century hermit who is buried in a restored chapel in the private grounds of a coastguard station on the cliffs. There are regular boat trips in season from Porthstinian to nearby Ramsey Island, a wildlife refuge and seal colony, and to other parts of the coast.

From Porthstinian you can set off on a wonderful 6½-mile coastal walk around the headland to Caerfai Bay, taking in the inlet of Porthclais (St David's old harbour) and St Non's Bay. Non was the mother of David. According to legend, David was born during a great storm around AD520 on the slopes above St Non's Bay, a spot marked by the ruins of a chapel of obscure origins. A small statue of St Non stands nearby, close to a holy well. A second chapel on the headland is part of St Non's Retreat, a centre for spiritual renewal.

Places to visit

St David's

Marine Life Centre
Tel (01437) 721665 C
Over 70 species of local marine life set within an aquarium of rocks, caves and large 'wreck' tank.

Oceanarium
Tel (01437) 720453 C
Sea aquarium with spectacular 9.25m-(30ft-) long panoramic tank and shark and ray tank with upstairs viewing gallery.

St David's Bishop's Palace
Tel (01437) 720517 C
Echoes of its former splendour still remain, especially in its multi-arched parapets.

St David's Cathedral
Medieval craftsmanship of the highest order. Beautifully located in grassy hollow.

St David's Farm Park (off B4583 on north-eastern outskirts)
Tel (01437) 721601 C
A rare breeds survival centre. Shire horses, farm trail, playground.

St Non's Chapel F
Ruins in beautiful setting overlooking the sea.

St David's Cathedral

St David, Wales's patron saint

Places to visit

Saundersfoot

Nearby

Folly Farm, Begelly, Kilgetty
Tel (01834) 812731 C
Popular family attraction based at large working dairy farm. Milking parlour, animal pens, museum, children's indoor and outdoor play areas, paddock, trailer rides, nature trail.

Saundersfoot

Stepaside Bird and Animal Park
Tel (01834) 843102 C
See many animals and birds, including crocodiles, meercats, owls and giant frogs. Falcon flying displays, adventure playground.

Stepaside Craft Village
Tel (01834) 811686 F
Variety of individual craft cabins in woodland setting. Picnic sites, woodland walks.

Places to visit

Skenfrith

Skenfrith Castle F
A key border defence, one of the 'Three Castles'.

Puffins on Skomer Island

Saundersfoot

Map Ref **B4**

Saundersfoot's capacious harbour is one of the most popular sailing and watersports centres in South Wales, allowing instant access to the waters of Carmarthen Bay. The resort itself is also deservedly popular. A long sandy beach stretches away from the quayside, close to all the amenities. Sea fishing is excellent – either from the harbour wall, shore or boat.

Wiseman's Bridge, a little way along the coast, has a small, steep beach on which the D-Day landings were rehearsed, watched by Winston Churchill. Landwards, Saundersfoot is almost encircled by wooded hills. At Stepaside 1½ miles to the north there is evidence which throws light on a very different Saundersfoot to the resort of today. In the 19th century, Saundersfoot was an exporting port for the mines of the south Pembrokeshire coalfield; and deep in the woods are the remains of one of those mines – the Grove Colliery – together with remnants of a 19th-century ironworks.

Skenfrith

Map Ref **H4**

This border village north-west of Monmouth is the home of one of the 'Three Castles' of the Welsh border. Together with Grosmont Castle and White Castle, Skenfrith controlled a stretch of borderland that was strategically important in medieval times. The original earth-and-timber castle here, put up to guard a river crossing, was replaced in stone in the early 13th century. The 'new' castle was built to a bold, simple plan influenced by the style of the French fortresses of that period. Skenfrith's well-preserved rectangular outer walls and corner towers contain its most dominant feature, a circular keep standing on a grassy enclosure.

The castle, interesting old church and peaceful village stand beside a loop in the River Monnow deep in undisturbed border country.

Skomer, Skokholm and Grassholm Islands

Map Ref **A4**

These strange-sounding islands have Norse placenames, a legacy from the times when Viking invaders plundered these shores. The islands are now internationally important sea-bird sanctuaries. The largest, and easiest to reach, is Skomer, a short boat trip from Martin's Haven (see Marloes entry). The island, which has one of the finest sea-bird populations in North-west Europe, is also a seal colony and home to a unique species of vole.

Britain's first bird observatory was established on Skokholm in 1933. Like Skomer, 2 miles to the north, it is a nature reserve of international repute. Grassholm is a tiny outcrop of cliffs 10 miles offshore. Every square metre of its surface seems to be covered with gannets. Its breeding population of about 30,000 pairs is reputed to be one of the world's largest gannet colonies.

Regular boat trips operate in season to Skomer. Access to Skokholm and Grassholm is much more limited (please enquire at local Tourist Information Centres for details).

Solva

Map Ref **A4**

Lower Solva is a picture-postcard village. Pristine cottages cluster around green hillsides and a snug quay sheltered from the open seas by a ½-mile tidal inlet. Solva is the safest, most sheltered port along this stretch of the coast. Its harbour brought the village prosperity as a trading port in the great days of seafaring. Solva enjoyed worldwide nautical links – the port was even used by boats which left for America with cargoes of Welsh emigrants paying £3 10 shillings per person.

Lower Solva's harbour now plays host to pleasure craft. Some of its cottages and substantial merchants' houses have been converted to craft shops; indeed, there is an exceptionally good range of such shops here, stocking high-quality – and highly individualistic – items ranging from ceramics to clothing. To appreciate Solva's sheltered location, follow the footpath from the harbour along the eastern side of the inlet. The walk, part of the long-distance Pembrokeshire Coast Path, winds its way along a grassy hillside to a point above the open seas.

The harbour, Solva

Places to visit

Solva

Nearby
Middle Mill (1 mile north-east of Solva)
Tel **(01437) 721112** F
Woollen mill specializing in carpets, tapestry and floor rugs in traditional and contemporary designs.

Southerndown

Map Ref **F6**

Dunraven Bay at Southerndown is one of the few places along a precipitous, cliff-backed coast where you can get down to the sea. A road leads down to an attractive sandy beach sheltering in rare break in the cliffs. The cliffs are part of the unspoilt Glamorgan Heritage Coast, a 14-mile stretch of dramatic shoreline between Porthcawl in the west and Aberthaw near Llantwit Major in the east.

There is a Heritage Coast visitor centre near the beach at Dunraven Bay. From the centre there is access to a 23-hectare (56-acre) stretch of sloping parklands which belonged to the demolished Dunraven Castle which stood on the headland above.

Places to visit

Southerndown
Glamorgan Heritage Coast Centre
Tel **(01656) 880157** F
Information and displays on coastline and wildlife.

Stackpole

Map Ref **B5**

The hamlet of Stackpole stands a little way inland from some of the finest coastal scenery in Pembrokeshire. Stackpole Quay is a tiny stone jetty, reputedly the smallest harbour in Britain, from which limestone was once shipped. Much of the land here is held by the National Trust. From the car park on the site of a former limestone quarry you can walk south across the grassy headlands to Barafundle Bay, a superb, secluded sandy beach backed by dunes.

If you have come this far, then you must walk a little further to Stackpole Head, a dizzily spectacular promontory and sea-bird colony jutting out uncompromisingly into the sea. But take care, especially on a windy day. The drops are steep!

Southerndown beach

Scenic Drives

The views along the A4069 north of Brynaman are enough to revive spirits deflated by the frustration of modern-day motoring. This glorious route, which winds its way across the empty landscapes of the Black Mountain, is one of the many scenic roads in South Wales. Stop off at the car park and viewpoint near the A4069's summit for marvellous panoramas looking northwards into the mountainous heart of Wales.

The views from the Heol Senni road are just as spectacular. Follow the minor country road north from the village of Ystradfellte across the lonely, windswept moors of Fforest Fawr. Suddenly, the road hairpins down a steep slope to a green, sheltered valley below.

Another not-to-be-missed route in the Brecon Beacons National Park is the remote road between Abergavenny and Hay-on-Wye. Heading north, turn off the A465 at Llanfihangel Crucorney and drive past Llanthony Priory. From here, the road narrows as it climbs up into the high country of Hay Bluff, where the clear-day views seem to go on forever. But please heed our advice. At busy times in summer and at all holiday weekends it should not be attempted, for the road is exceedingly narrow in parts, with few passing places.

The most memorable approach to the Rhondda is along the A4061 Rhigos road from Hirwaun which climbs over a formidable north-facing escarpment before plunging down into the tightly packed confines of Treherbert and Treorchy. Stay on the A4061 beyond Treorchy for more spectacle as the road climbs out of the valley. At its lofty junction with the A4107 – from which Treorchy looks like a toy-town – you can

either drive west into the Afan Valley or south through the Ogmore Valley.

The South Wales Valleys are a surprisingly fertile source of scenic roads. Quite apart from the Forestry Commission's scenic drive at Cwmcarn, there are many roads which loop over the valleys' roller-coaster landscape of high mountains and deep vales.

These are just some of South Wales's scenic routes. There are many others – through the Brechfa Forest, for example, or the Preseli Hills, or the rolling borderlands. Get yourself a good map, call in at a Tourist Information Centre for advice, and discover South Wales's scenic highways and byways.

Storey Arms

Map Ref **F4**

There's nothing at Storey Arms apart from a car park and outdoor pursuits centre, yet it is a very well known – and popular – spot. The reason lies in its location, in the heart of the Brecon Beacons National Park at the top of a 439m (1440ft) pass through the mountains and close to the highest peaks in South Wales.

Pont ar Daf at Storey Arms is the place where most people set off to walk to the Beacons' distinctive, flat-topped 886m (2907ft) summit of Pen-y-fan – and therein lies a problem, for the footpath along the flanks of the mountain has become badly eroded. There are other, less well-used – and more interesting – approaches to the summit, so get out your Ordnance Survey map and try not to follow the crowds. Storey Arms was named after landowner Story Maskelyne. It was never, as its name implies, an inn.

Storey Arms lies in the heart of the Beacons

Swansea

Map Ref **E5**

Dylan Thomas was born in Swansea. In one of his often-quoted descriptions, he called Swansea an 'ugly, lovely town'. Things have changed since Thomas's time; he'd hardly recognize the Swansea of today. The 'ugly, lovely' place of his boyhood now boasts one of Europe's most stunning and successful waterfront developments. And the town has become a city, second only in status and size to the capital of Cardiff.

The Swansea of today is a breezy, self-confident city by the sea. There's an appealing mix of influences at work here. The sandy beaches of Swansea Bay are just a few minutes away from the modern shopping centre, the old docklands have been rejuvenated with great imagination and flair, there are green areas of parkland and gardens close to the centre, and the city, while looking to the future, retains a sense of Welshness that is lacking in cosmopolitan Cardiff.

The Swansea which Dylan Thomas might still recognize lives on at the covered market. Although housed in a modern building in the heart of the city centre, Swansea Market is as traditional as they come. Its fresh foods are superb – you can buy anything from the best Welsh lamb to laverbread, that unique Welsh delicacy (a sort of puréed seaweed) which looks – and tastes – like nothing else. Swansea Market is also the place to buy seafoods, including cockles freshly picked from the nearby Penclawdd beds.

The city's attractive new face is to be found along the waterfront. In the 19th century, Swansea was caught up in the great period of industrial expansion, serving as a port for the local metal-producing industries. The docklands fell into sad decline in the 20th century, only to be reborn again in the last few decades when the city renewed its links with the sea by building its Maritime Quarter.

Its centrepiece is a 600-berth marina at the old South Dock. But the area is much more than a place for keeping

Places to visit

Swansea
Brangwyn Hall, The Guildhall
(off Oystermouth Road ¾ mile from the city centre)
Tel (01792) 635489
Hosts many large-scale musical events.

Clyne Valley Country Park (off Mumbles Road 2½ miles south-west of city centre)
Tel (01792) 298637 F
Varied park of 293 hectares (725 acres) which combines natural beauty with industrial heritage. Woodland trails, footpath and cycleway.

Swansea Bay (top), city centre (right) and market (left)

Dylan Thomas Theatre, Gloucester Place
Tel (01792) 473238
Regular productions throughout year.

Glynn Vivian Art Gallery, Alexandra Road
Tel (01792) 655006 F
Fascinating collection of paintings plus exquisite Swansea pottery and porcelain; also European ceramics and glass.

(continued overleaf)

The marina, Swansea

Places to visit

Swansea

Grand Theatre, Singleton Street
Tel (01792) 475715
Beautifully refurbished – one of
Britain's finest regional theatres. Wide
range of productions.

Maritime and Industrial Museum,
Maritime Quarter
Tel (01792) 650351 F
Exciting museum housed in former
warehouse tells the story of Swansea's
development. Boat and transport
displays. Some 'exhibits' – a lightship,
steam tug, etc – moored on quayside
outside. Museum also contains a fully
operational woollen mill. Tramshed
annexe dedicated to the Mumbles
Railway, the world's first passenger-
carrying railway which ran along
seafront.

Plantasia, Parc Tawe, North Dock
Tel (01792) 474555 C
Giant, futuristically designed hothouse
with three computer-controlled
climatic zones – arid, tropical and
humid. 5000 plants of 850 varieties.
Aviary contains exotic birds.

boats. The Maritime Quarter is a living part of the city.
The marina is surrounded by attractive residential
developments, shops, eating places, a museum, leisure
centre and hotel; and the entire complex is enlivened by a
host of architectural features which delight the eye. Along
the seafront, for example, there is a crazy lighthouse and
observatory tower, while elsewhere you'll
come across stone carvings, painted doors
and copper statues which tell the story of
Swansea's heritage sometimes directly, at
other times obliquely. Swansea is still a
working port. The Swansea–Cork ferry is
one of the services which uses the
commercial docks to the east of the
Maritime Quarter.

Dylan Thomas, Swansea's most famous son

Back in the city centre – which suffered
severe bomb damage in World War II –
there are a few survivors from the old
town. Salubrious Passage off Wind Street
is a narrow Dickensian alleyway. Close by
is the unusually named 'No Sign Bar', one
of the oldest properties in Swansea. A
lengthy explanation of its name – too complicated to
repeat here! – appears on the front of the premises.

The oldest building of all really looks its age. This is the
ragged ruin of Swansea Castle, a medieval misfit standing
amongst modern buildings near the shopping centre. The
castle's northern block served as a grim debtors' prison
which was closed in 1858 after
protests about its scandalous
conditions.

Swansea can be proud of its
patronage of museums and the arts.
Swansea Museum, founded in 1838
and housed in a grand, Classically
inspired building near the Maritime
Quarter, has the distinction of being
Wales's first museum. The Glynn
Vivian Art Gallery, at the opposite
end of the city centre, was opened in
1911 thanks to the generosity of the
prosperous Vivian family, who made
their fortune as 19th-century
industrialists.

A statue of Dylan Thomas stands
at the approach to the marina, next to

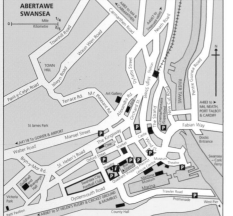

the small Dylan Thomas Theatre. Thomas lived in Swansea's Uplands district west of the city centre. His birthplace, 5 Cwmdonkin Drive, is a turn-of-the-century semi-detached house indistinguishable from all the rest apart from its blue plaque bearing the poet's name. Devotees of Thomas will be familiar with his reminiscences of his childhood haunt, Cwmdonkin Park. This peaceful park, set in a wooded dell, contains a memorial inscribed with lines from *Fern Hill*, one of his most beautiful poems.

The 'long and splendidly curving shore' of Swansea Bay, which Thomas could see from his Uplands perch, links the city to Mumbles, a charming little resort and watersports centre (see separate entry). Swansea's Guildhall, which stands near the seafront below the Uplands, is the home of the Brangwyn Panels, a stunning series of murals originally destined for the House of Lords. The 18 panels, based on the theme of the British Empire and bursting with life and colour, were painted by Sir Frank Brangwyn in the 1920s and '30s. They decorate the walls of the Brangwyn Hall, which is the focal point of the prestigious Swansea Festival, held each autumn.

A footpath and cycleway runs from the Maritime Quarter all the way along the seafront to Mumbles, a distance of over 5 miles. Stop off on the way at two beautiful stretches of greenery. Singleton Park is a large parkland with a boating lake, children's play areas and botanic gardens. Nearby Clyne Gardens, adjacent to Clyne Valley Country Park, is famous for its azaleas and rhododendrons.

Talgarth

Map Ref G3

This sleepy country town deserves a second look. St Gwendoline's Church has a memorial to Hywel Harris, a remarkable man who led the Methodist Revival in Wales. An inscription on the memorial recalls Harris's experience in the church in 1735 when he 'felt suddenly my heart melting within me like wax before the fire with love to God my Saviour'.

The centre of Talgarth is dominated by its old Town Hall. The oldest building of all stands opposite – a strange-looking medieval tower, topped by a stone-tiled roof.

Harris founded a religious settlement known as the 'Connexion' at nearby Trefeca. Its members in many ways anticipated later social experiments by farming the land and living a strictly communal life.

Talley

Map Ref E3

Hidden away in the hills, tranquil Talley is rooted in religion. Two religious sites stand next to its twin lakes. The oldest is Talley Abbey, founded in the late 12th century. A tall archway, part of its centre tower, is the most striking feature of this evocative ruin on the shores of Talley's southern lake.

Close by is St Michael's Church, dating from 1773. The church was built to a most unusual plan. Its lack of any central aisle (a consequence of its two entrance doors) and interior of box pews give it the look of a Welsh chapel rather than an Anglican place of worship.

In the lanes south of Talley is the delightful hamlet of Cwmdu, where the National Trust has preserved a row of cottages, the village shop and tiny pub.

Places to visit

Swansea

Swansea Castle, Castle Street
Ruins of 14th-century fortress. View from surrounding area only.

Swansea Leisure Centre, Oystermouth Road
Tel (01792) 649126 C
Superb pool with 'beach area', variety of aquaslides and wave machine. Jacuzzi, sauna, sunbeds, squash, badminton and other sports. Very popular – a top South Wales attraction.

Swansea Museum, Victoria Road
Tel (01792) 653763 C
Wide range of exhibits covering geology, history and natural history. Exceptional ceramics collection reflecting Swansea's 18th- and 19th-century porcelain and pottery industry.

Taliesin Arts Centre, University of Wales Swansea
Tel (01792) 296883
Theatre, music, dance, film and the visual arts. Egypt Centre museum.

Tŷ Llên, Somerset Place
Tel (01792) 463892 F
The National Literature Centre for Wales. Exhibition galleries, bookshop, theatre (C for performances).

Places to visit

Talgarth

Nearby
Bronllys Castle F
A massive, chimney-like single round tower crowning an exceptionally steep hill. Built in the mid-13th century.

Hywel Harris Museum, Trefeca
Tel (01874) 711423 F
Fascinating little museum to a fascinating man. Housed at Harris's original settlement, now a Presbyterian College.

Places to visit

Talley

Talley Abbey C
Ruins in beautiful lakeside setting.

Tranquil Talley Abbey

Talybont on Usk

Map Ref **F4**

In the hills above the Talybont reservoir

The village, despite its name, does not stand on the Usk but on the banks of another waterway, the Monmouthshire and Brecon Canal. The Usk flows in a broad, beautiful vale ¹/₂ mile from the centre of Talybont; the canal is carved out on a shoulder of land above the rooftops, though with good access – much appreciated by holidaying canal cruisers – from the towpath to the village's old inns.

Poet Henry Vaughan (1621–95), whose family came from Tretower Court (see Crickhowell entry), lies buried at nearby Llansantffraid Church. The minor road south of Talybont travels along the banks of the scenic 2-mile-long Talybont reservoir, a nature reserve noted for its birdlife. Past the reservoir, the road climbs through the Talybont Forest and over the mountains on its way to Pontsticill (see Pontsticill entry).

Picturesque Tenby on Pembrokeshire's south coast

Places to visit

Tenby

Silent World Aquarium, Mayfield Drive, Narberth Road
Tel (01834) 844498 C
Pembrokeshire's sea, river and lake creatures. Rock pool touch-tank for the children. Wildlife art gallery.

Tenby Castle, Castle Hill F
Scattered remains of mid-12th-century headland fortress.

Tenby Museum, Castle Hill
Tel (01834) 842809 C
Features Tenby's maritime history and growth as a fashionable resort. Natural history displays. Excellent picture gallery with works by Augustus John, Tenby's most famous son, and his sister Gwen.

Tudor Merchant's House, Quay Hill
Tel (01834) 842279 C
Well-preserved house which shows how prosperous merchants lived when Tenby was a busy trading port. Original fireplaces, chimneys and floor beams. Wall frescoes.

Tenby

Map Ref **B5**

Tenby presents an idealized picture of a seaside resort. Pastel-shaded Georgian houses crowd around a pretty harbourside, while the streets above are a medieval jumble of narrow thoroughfares encircled by ancient town walls. Unlike many popular seaside centres, Tenby's period charm remains undimmed by the passage of time or the excesses of commercialization. It is a delightful place which still lives up to its 19th-century description as a resort 'whose every view is picturesque in the extreme'. The only drawback is its incompatibility with modern traffic. Use the large car parks on the fringe of the old town. Don't expect to park your car in Tenby's confined, historic centre during the summer.

Tenby's past is embodied in its Welsh name, Dinbych y Pysgod (Little Fort of the Fish), a reference both to its medieval castle and to the fishing boats that once sailed from the harbour. Tenby was also an early resort, attracting visitors from the latter part of the 18th century when sea-bathing first became fashionable.

Today's visitors come for much the same reasons. Tenby's beautiful beaches spread themselves out beneath steep cliffs. The 1¹/₂-mile South Sands and shorter North Sands are separated by a grassy headland which contains the ruins of a medieval castle, an imposing Victorian memorial and the town's museum. The views from this panoramic perch are marvellous. The headland overlooks a huge stretch of the Pembrokeshire coast, Caldy Island and – a little closer to home – St Catherine's Island directly below, a tidal outcrop crowned by a squat Victorian fort.

The castle was only a part of the town's defences. The historic centre of Tenby, a maze of passageways and narrow streets, is enclosed within a ring of walls which, unlike the castle, are exceptionally well preserved. Dating from the 13th century, they still stand to their full height in parts – along South Parade, for example, where you can see the arrow-slits. The walls were protected by a series of towers and fortified gateways, the most famous of which is the Five Arches (there are, in fact, six archways around this heavily defended gateway) along St Florence Parade.

Within the town there are many fine old buildings. None is more interesting than the Tudor Merchant's House, a tall, three-storeyed late 15th-century building which is probably the oldest surviving dwelling in Tenby. Look out also around the harbour for the little 'Fisherman's Church' of St Julian's Chapel and Laston House, location of Tenby's original swimming baths and assembly rooms (the Greek inscription above its doorway means 'The sea washes away all ills'). St Mary's Church, whose soaring 46m (152ft) steeple dominates Tudor Square, is a grand place of worship dating from the 13th century. Its lavish proportions, decorative features and monuments reflect Tenby's past prosperity as a trading port.

Tenby's harbour is still a busy place in summer. The most popular boat trips are those that travel to nearby Caldy Island. You can spend the whole day on this lovely 1½-mile-long island, exploring its coastline, looking out for sea-birds and seals, and visiting its religious sites which include a medieval church and Cistercian abbey.

Activities at the resort include golf (an 18-hole links course), fishing and watersports. There is an indoor swimming pool in Marsh Road. The De Valence Pavilion is Tenby's largest venue for shows and entertainments.

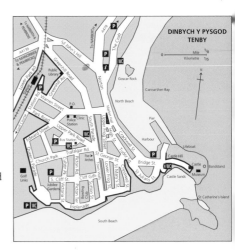

Places to visit

Tenby

Nearby

Caldy Island Monastery C
Conducted tours by the monks, who produce Caldy Island perfume from the island's gorse and wild flowers.

Carswell Medieval House N
(in farmyard 1 mile east of St Florence) F
Off-the-beaten-track little two-storeyed building. Limited access.

The Five Arches gateway, Tenby

Great Wedlock Dinosaur Experience, Gumfreston
Tel (01834) 845272 C
'Hands on' prehistory for all the family in country park setting. Dinosaur trail, activity centre, adventure playground.

Heatherton Country Sports Park, St Florence
Tel (01646) 651025 C
Pitch and putt, floodlit golf driving range, archery, laser clay-pigeon shooting, go-karts, children's play area.

Manor House Wildlife and Leisure Park, St Florence
Tel (01646) 651201 C
5-hectare (12-acre) wooded park with birds and animals, aquarium and reptiles. Model railway exhibition, falconry demonstrations, beautiful gardens with floral displays, children's play area with go-karts and giant slide.

Take a boat trip to Caldy Island

Three Cliffs on Gower's south coast

Three Cliffs Bay

Map Ref **D5**

This is possibly the most famous beauty spot on the Gower Peninsula. Three triangular crags give this lovely sandy bay its name. The beach lies on the mouth of Pennard Pill, a small river flowing into the sea from Parkmill. You can walk to the bay from Penmaen or Parkmill (see Parkmill entry).

Places to visit

Tintern

Tintern Abbey
Tel (01291) 689251 C
Extensive ruins dominated by towering remains of abbey church, built with patronage of Roger Bigod III, Lord of Chepstow, between 1269 and 1301. Remains of chapter house, infirmary, warming house, dining hall and other buildings. Exhibition.

Tintern Old Station
Tel (01291) 689566 F
One-time Victorian railway station imaginatively transformed into visitor centre. Old handbills, posters, goods labels, photographs of locomotives, countryside exhibition. Leafy railway trail alongside river plus other walks. Children can work signals. Play area, picnic tables.

Tintern

Map Ref **H4**

This picturesque village in the Wye Valley is best known for its ruined abbey, which inspired a much-quoted poem by William Wordsworth. It has been attracting sightseers ever since two-day trips down the Wye were organized for well-heeled tourists in the 18th century. The ruins are as magnificent a spectacle as ever. Open to the skies, the lofty walls have such graceful lines that in spite of their size they seem light and insubstantial, as if they might float away at any second. Birds flutter in and out of the bare windows and around the pillars; the abbey seems as much a work of nature as of man.

Tintern Abbey belonged to the Cistercians, who lived an austere life and were known as the 'white monks' because they wore habits of undyed wool. It was founded in 1131 and dissolved in 1536. The Cistercians ruthlessly felled trees in order to cultivate the land, but today the forests around Tintern are rigorously preserved and provide a diversity of walks. Tintern itself has a good range of antique and craft shops.

The Wye Valley is beautiful at any time of year, the pristine freshness of the woodlands in spring contrasting with the rich hues of autumn. The section in which Tintern stands has been declared an Area of Outstanding Natural Beauty. Tintern is a good base from which to explore the many footpaths which run through the surrounding hills and woods. The best starting point for walkers is the countryside centre based at the old railway station.

Tintern Abbey

Places to visit

Tredegar

Parc Bryn Bach (on western outskirts of Tredegar)
Tel (01495) 711816 F
243-hectare (600-acre) park. Walks, fishing, watersports, visitor centre.

Nearby
Drenewydd Museum, Bute Town
Tel (01685) 843039 C
Museum in two former ironworks' cottages. Victorian garden.

Parc Cwm Darran (on minor road 2½ miles south of Rhymney)
Tel (01443) 875557 F
Country park with invigorating 'open' feel about it. Lakes, fishing, walking, cycleway, visitor centre, adventure playground, picnic areas.

Tredegar

Map Ref **G4**

The clock tower in the town centre looks like a refugee from a bowling green of a South Coast resort. The 22m (72ft) structure is made of iron, a reminder that Tredegar once depended on ironmaking for its living. Another unexpected sight is the village of Bute Town, 2 miles to the west. This attractive, well-planned 'model' village of orderly streets was built by a philanthropic ironmaster for his workers in 1802–3. The grand Bedwellty House, set in parkland a short distance from Tredegar's town centre, was the former home of a local ironmaster.

Tredegar stands on the northern rim of the valleys, close to the beautiful countryside of the Brecon Beacons National Park. This description applies as much to parts of the valleys as it does to the nearby Beacons. Parc Bryn Bach, for example, is an extensive stretch of grassland and woodland ranged around a man-made lake. A former industrial wasteland, it is an example of the remarkable transformations that have been achieved in the valleys by environmental improvement schemes. The same applies to Parc Cwm Darran, further south. It is difficult to believe that a colliery once stood in this scenic spot.

Usk

Map Ref **H4**

Usk stands in a pretty rural setting on the looping river of the same name, famous for its salmon fishing. Usk's broad square gives the little town a sense of spaciousness more typical of an English than Welsh settlement. In common with many border towns, Usk was a Norman stronghold. The remains of a medieval castle have been partially converted into a private house.

The town is noted for its summer floral displays and interesting old buildings, including an Italianate Town Hall. An ancient malt barn houses the Gwent Rural Life Museum, which portrays border country life from Victorian times to the end of World War II. The churches at nearby Llangwm Uchaf and Bettws-newydd have outstanding, elaborately carved rood screens dating from the late 15th century.

Whitland

Map Ref **C4**

This small market town is remembered in the history books as the 10th-century meeting place of an assembly – one of the first of its kind in Britain – which was an important early step in the development of legal systems. Welsh leader Hywel Dda (Hywel the Good) held an assembly here which established a unified legal code for Wales.

Ystradfellte

Map Ref **F4**

The hamlet of Ystradfellte is much better known than its size might suggest. Its fame lies in its location in a strange corner of the Brecon Beacons National Park where there are wooded gorges, waterfalls, caves and pot-holes instead of bare-sloped, open mountainsides. The reason for the change in the landscape is the underlying limestone rock around Ystradfellte, which replaces the old red sandstones from which the main bulk of the Beacons are formed.

At Porth yr Ogof south of Ystradfellte a gargantuan cave mouth, possibly the largest in Wales, swallows up the River Mellte. The river reappears $\frac{1}{4}$ mile downstream. You can follow the riverbank for about a mile to a series of spectacular waterfalls. The first is Sgwd Clun-gwyn (White Meadow Fall), followed by Sgwd Isaf Clun-gwyn (Lower White Meadow Fall) – sometimes called a 'miniature Niagara' – and Sgwd y Pannwr (Fall of the Fuller).

The most famous fall of them all is Sgwd yr Eira (Fall of Snow) on the River Hepste, which joins the Mellte downstream from Sgwd y Pannwr. This waterfall's overhang is so acute that you can walk behind its curtain of water without getting wet. Sgwd yr Eira is also accessible across the moorland from Penderyn.

A note of caution: keep to the main paths, for some of the ground is steep and unstable; and do not enter any caves unless you are properly equipped.

Places to visit

Usk

Gwent Rural Life Museum
Tel (01291) 673777 C
Thousands of exhibits, including vintage farming machinery. Victorian kitchen, rural crafts.

Usk Castle. In private ownership
Viewing by appointment
Please contact Mr Humphreys, Castle House, Usk (tel 01291-672563).

Nearby
Brecon Court Deer Farm and Cwrt-y-Brychan Vineyard, Llansoy
Tel (01291) 650366 C
Red deer herd and vineyard. Free wine tasting. Picnic areas, farm shop.

Places to visit

Whitland

Hywel Dda Gardens
Tel (01994) 240867 F
Interpretive and information centre based on the king's pioneering legal work.

Nearby
Grove Land Adventure World
nr St Clear's
Tel (01994) 231440/231181 C
Wide range of rides and attractions including bumper boats, pedaloes, go-karts and laser clay pigeon shoot.

Pemberton's Victorian Chocolates
Llanboidy
Tel (01994) 448768 C **(demonstrations)**
See gourmet chocolates being made in a beautiful 200-year-old store barn. Shop.

The falls at Ystradfellte

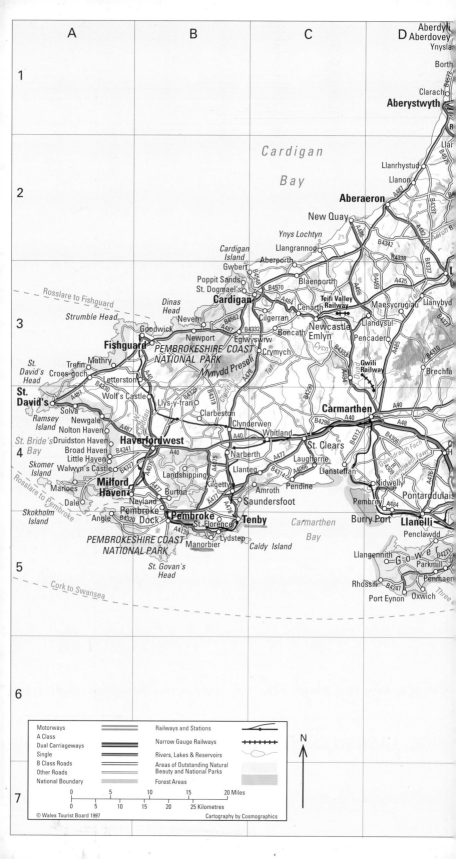